PRACTISING SOCIAL WORK SOCIOLOGICALLY

PRACTISING SOCIAL WORK SOCIOLOGICALLY

A THEORETICAL APPROACH FOR NEW TIMES

PRISCILLA DUNK-WEST AND

FIONA VERITY

First published 2018 by
PALGRAVE

Palgrave in the UK is an imprint of Macmillan Publishers Limited, registered in England, company number 785998, of 4 Crinan Street, London, N1 9XW.

Palgrave® and Macmillan® are registered trademarks in the United States, the United Kingdom, Europe and other countries.

ISBN 978–1–137–54807–8 paperback

This book is printed on paper suitable for recycling and made from fully managed and sustained forest sources. Logging, pulping and manufacturing processes are expected to conform to the environmental regulations of the country of origin.

A catalogue record for this book is available from the British Library.

A catalog record for this book is available from the Library of Congress.

CONTENTS

List of figures and tables   viii

Acknowledgements   ix

1 Introduction   **1**
Social work is not unversed in sociology   4
About this book   5
How to read this book   7

2 Who Are We and What Do We Do?   **8**
Introduction   8
Jane Addams (1860–1935)   10
Summary   13
Alice Salomon (1872–1948)   13
Summary   16
Clare Britton Winnicott (1906–1984)   17
Summary   19
Practice in a global world   19
Conclusions   22
Practising social work sociologically   22

3 Imagination in Practising Social Work Sociologically   **23**
Introduction   23
Imagination   24
Empathy and imagination   27
Imagining social objectives   29
C. Wright Mills' sociological imagination   34
Conclusions   35
Practising social work sociologically   36

4 Imaginative Sensibilities and Habits   **38**
Introduction   38
Social work in an 'iron cage'   38
An order to support imaginative habits   42
An order for creative and imaginative habits in social work   44
Curiosity   44
Drawing comparisons and making connections   47
Surrounding   50
Conclusions   52
Practising social work sociologically   52

5   Self, Agency and Structure   **53**
Introduction   53
Identity/self   53
Identity categories   54
Reflexivity in social work   55
Symbolic interactionism and the self   56
Agency   61
Social structure   62
Conclusions   63
Practising social work sociologically   64

6   Social Relationships and 'Capital'   **65**
Introduction   65
Public narrative of the individual   66
Social ties and bonds   72
Conclusions   78
Practising social work sociologically   78

7   Time and Space in Social Work   **80**
Time and space in contemporary life   81
Nation as space   83
Historical perspectives   86
Time as a constraint to social work practice   91
Conclusions   92
Practising social work sociologically   93

8   Organisations and Sociological Social Work   **94**
Introduction   94
Gareth Morgan's organisational metaphors   96
Using Morgan's organisational metaphors to think about social work
    and organisations   98
Morgan's metaphor: organisation as 'machines'   98
Social work and organisations: a machine?   99
Morgan's metaphor: organisation as 'organism'   100
Social work and organisations: an organism?   101
Morgan's metaphor: organisation as 'brain'   104
Social work and organisations: a brain?   104
Morgan's metaphor: organisation as 'instrument of domination'   106
Social work and organisations: as 'instruments of domination'?   107
Conclusions   108
Practising social work sociologically   109

9   Using Research in Practice   **110**
What is research?   110
Objective knowledge?   111
The research question   115
Social research methodology and methods   116

	Methods	118
	New kinds of research in new times	119
	Big data	120
	Conclusions	120
	Practising social work sociologically	121
10	**Conclusions and Future Directions**	**122**
	Introduction	122
	Tools for practising social work sociologically	123
	Future directions	126
	References	128
	Index	136

LIST OF FIGURES AND TABLES

Figures

3.1 Aspects of a social work imagination 33
3.2 Imagination and creativity in practising social work sociologically 36
4.1 Sand Drawing: Hope 41
4.2 Shaking up thinking 45
4.3 Shaking up thinking 49
6.1 *Sad Woman* by Lucy Littleford 67
6.2 *Sad Women* by Lucy Littleford 74
7.1 Spatial placement of human rights in social work 82
7.2 Thinking about nation 86
9.1 The stick 113
9.2 Stick swords 114

Tables

5.1 Social Structure, Theoretical Traditions and Theorists 63
7.1 Spatial Placement of Human Rights in Social Work 92
10.1 Domains and Tools for Practising Social Work Sociologically 126

ACKNOWLEDGEMENTS

To my social work students, past, present and future: thank you for keeping me engaged with my sociological imagination. Peter from Palgrave has been terrific to work with: thank you for your enthusiasm and patience for this project. To Penny and Jamie, for your eternal support and laughter: thank you. A big thank you to Maddison and Lucy for the photography and artwork: I hope you like seeing your work in print. Kylie Turner – as always – has been a brilliant support. Thanks to Margi for being a beautiful human. Last, but by no means least, to Blake and Paxton – for keeping my mind alive and curious about the world.

Priscilla Dunk-West

I am grateful to my social work colleague Elizabeth Becker for her engagement in lively conversations on the chapters on social work history, imagination and creativity and the organisational context of practice, which she read in draft form. Gratitude to Community Health Onkaparinga (CHO) for permission to use a photograph in Chapter 3. I also thank our editor Peter from Palgrave; the reviewers of our earlier book, *Sociological Social Work*, whose penetrating critiques pushed the boundaries of my thinking; and the anonymous reviewers of this book for their time and thoughtful comments.

Fiona Verity

ACKNOWLEDGMENTS

1

Introduction

Draw yourself away from your everyday existence. You may be reading this book in a library, at home or during a ride on public transport. Think about floating away from where you are right now, up and above your location, above your local community, above your country, above seas and landscapes, and imagine that you are able to travel into space. Now imagine that you are a visitor in space, spending time on the International Space Station (ISS) as it orbits the globe and that on board is a machine called the 'Social Viewer'. This machine allows you to observe and compare social worlds as the Space Station does its rotation around the Earth. What might you see from this incredibly distant perspective? How is the world characterised?

You will begin to see patterns in time and space. Patterns which shape people's everyday experiences. Patterns which are located in culture and societies. It might be generational patterns in the use of social media; robotic technologies and changes in industrial processes and workplaces; the impact of climate change on people's security, health and roots; cities with regular daily rhythms and patterns of shopping and consumption; people engaging with friends, families and communities and the everyday rituals and activities within homes and households. What differences do you see between north and southern hemispheres; between and within countries and across cultures and cities, regions and rural locations? You will no doubt see similarities as well. Imagine that the 'Social Viewer' machine allows you to explore intersections between age, sexuality, class, gender, race and culture. What patterns come into focus? What puzzles you? Where are the inequalities and where is power? What if you could see back in time at the same time? What broader patterns might emerge? What national differences and similarities might there be? Imagine you encountered an alien on the space station and that you were asked to explain what being a human on Earth was like.

Such an approach to seeing social worlds follows the imagination of the sociologist C. W. Mills (1970), who laid out a means to think about and explore the intersection of the 'micro' world and the 'macro' social world across time past and time future. He called this process an exercise in using a 'sociological imagination'. Sociology is a scholarly pursuit which looks for patterns, consistencies and breaks, or discontinuities, in individual/group and community meanings and behaviours, to understand the role of societies in influencing them, and as well, how societies are reproduced and changed (Bauman and May, 2001). There are many sociologies, and while it is true to say that there is no 'one' sociology, it is important to recognise the central theme in this discipline. Sociology provides a range of theoretical perspectives which each have a set of epistemological standpoints. That is, each tradition in sociology stands on a foundation in which the relationship between the individual and social group, and their culture and society in a historical time is theorised.

In 2013 we worked together on a book called *Sociological Social Work* (Dunk-West and Verity, 2013), motivated by our own intentions to explore how social work could be better served by closer engagement with sociological ideas and ways of understanding the changing social world, as firm theoretical underpinnings of practice. We drew from the rich history that social work and sociology have together and presented theories which underlined synergies between these two perspectives. We defined sociological social work as:

> ... social work which is animated by a life-long sociological interpretative perspective. It is practiced by social workers able to engage their sociological sensibilities and requires knowledge about social work and sociological theories about the world and our day to day interactions, both with the people with whom we work and the agency/public policy context.
>
> (2013, p. 1)

and

> Sociological social work, we argue, ought to be used as a way to name and justify a kind of practice in which sociological theory comes together with social work aims. Sociological social work is also a sensibility: it marks a particular orientation which helps in addressing some of the key challenges which emerge in our changing world.
>
> (2013, p. 5)

Our focus was on a way of critically analysing, seeing and being that we believe has relevance across social work fields of practice. Throughout the book we traced sociological ideas with application to the use of the social work self, the organisational context in which social work takes place, social work values and ethics and contemporary social issues and challenges which impact on experiences of injustice and attainment of social justice. These include the complex impacts of economic inequalities and the workings of neo-liberal capitalism, the need for social solidarity and the contradictions for social justice based social work in a world dominated by individualistic objectives and techno-rational systems.

Building on our previous work, in this book we focus more directly on ideas and practices that can support a spirit and efficacy of a sociological social work which engages sociological thinking in practice. As you well know from your own social work practice or student placement, contemporary public policies have impacted deeply on the contexts and environments in which people live and work, and the provision, funding and organisational contexts of social welfare and social work. These public policies have changed the ways in which governments interact with people, communities and the market. In the United Kingdom, successive governments have reduced funds for the public sector and individualised services through policy measures such as personalisation approaches. Austerity measures have had profound impacts on economic and social wellbeing and hope, and economic inequalities are growing (Corlett and Clarke, 2017).

Our perspective is that with the sharp ascendency of right-wing values and practices across the globe, and ever present hardships for many, social work needs theoretical reference points which are strongly aligned with not only the interpersonal dimension to the work, but also to the political, economic and global structural conditions within which our work is located. Complexity, uncertainty and unpredictability are now key themes in contemporary social science and public policy literature. With the development of new kinds of social interaction and the pace and nature of social life changing, social workers can feel underprepared for the issues which they face in practice, particularly when holding on to theoretical traditions. This is not to say that the current theories used in social work do not provide social workers with the means to grapple with contemporary issues and complexity. Rather, social workers need to critically evaluate and update knowledge in relation to the external, organisational and social environments within which they work. For this task, we see sociological theory and a sociological approach marked by curiosity as vital aspects of social work practice.

Social work has an applied focus; we are there to contribute to making a difference. But of course, we are not absent in thinking, in using theory and concepts in our social work practice and in developing knowledge about social worlds and ourselves from practice experiences, research and through what we learn from the people we work with. In social work education, students learn about a range of social work theories. The role of theory in social work, historically, has had multiple functions. Firstly, theory helps social work distinguish itself from other disciplines and professions. Here, theory helps to sketch out a domain of thought and practice, and is used to underpin practice and a way of seeing the world. The range of theoretical perspectives in social work is far-reaching.

From practical suggestions about how to respond to client issues and support community development and policy change, to more philosophical questions about what it means to be a social worker, theories help navigate this terrain. One of the issues with social work theories is that students might choose a few theories which resonate with their ethical and value base and these theories can be useful to creating a social work identity, which, as Rogers might say, helps with *congruence*. Social workers can embed these chosen or favourite theories into their practice in an enduring fashion. This can fix a theoretical perspective to the point at which people begin to think of themselves as social workers – the educational moment in time when theories resonate often equates to hesitancy, years on, to move into new ways of thinking. What necessitates new ways of thinking? Why is it important to critically engage in theory? These questions we believe are important ones to keep asking.

Social work is not unversed in sociology

As we noted earlier in this introduction, the approach we present is not new in social work. William Schwartz sensibly reminds us, 'Professions have a way of moving periodically through eras of rediscovery in which an old truth comes alive with the vigor and freshness of a new idea' (1979, p. 14). We contend that connecting social work and sociology to be something of an 'old truth' (e.g., see Addams, ud; Davies, 1991; Sibeon, 1991; Lee, 1994; Dominelli, 1997; van Wormer, 2002; Cunningham and Cunningham, 2008; MacLean and Williams, 2012; Garrett, 2012; Shaw, 2014); one that has been with social work from the beginning and bounced along with the shifts in what knowledge is privileged in social work education and policy and practice settings. There is a tradition of social work writers and practitioners connecting sociological theory with social work knowledge and practice, for example, drawing on sociological theories about the nexus between power and knowledge, class, families and communities, organisations, ethnicity and race, gender relations, social analysis and social change (e.g., Bryson and Mowbray, 1981; Davies, 1991; Sibeon, 1991; Dominelli, 1997; Mullaly, 1997; Cunningham and Cunningham, 2008; Garrett, 2012; Shaw, 2014). Other writers have emphasised the use of sociological methods or approaches in social work practice, as a way to systematically explore and understand social worlds; knowledge to use in social work (e.g. Sibeon, 1991; Shaw, 2014).

There are plenty of examples of social workers who have worked in this tradition and encouraged this perspective. Jane Addams was an applied urban sociologist and social worker active in North America at the end of the nineteenth century and into the twentieth century. She contributed substantially to social work and sociological knowledge. MacLean and Williams note Jane Addams was a '...founding member of the American Sociological Society' (2012, p. 239). In the 1970s and 1980s, Marxist and feminist sociology informed radical and feminist social work. Twenty years ago, Dominelli (1997) directly positioned sociological social work as essential in building a scaffolding where a 'politics of practice' is shaped from sociological perspectives. More recently, Shaw (2014, p. 767) traces historical episodes of social work and sociology's 'inter-relationship' to outline a shape of a sociological social work. Both Dominelli and Shaw articulate a perspective on sociological social work.

About this book

This book aims to expand and extend our scholarship outlined in *Sociological Social Work* so that this approach is accessible to social work students and practitioners. We have included diagrams, visual depictions and exercises in this book in the hope that it represents an engaging resource designed to assist social workers in navigating the challenges of the contemporary world.

In Chapter 2 we trace the contours of a sociological perspective and approach in social work, back to a time when indeed social work and sociology were new practices. We trace these influences by looking through a window on the lives and work of three inspirational social workers, Alice Salomon, Jane Addams and Clare Winnicott, who contributed extensively to knowledge and practice. In telling something of our interpretation of their lives and work, we introduce the overall text. Each practised in ways that reflect a universal dimension to social work and the particularities of their context; an orientation which emerged from the social, cultural, economic and political context of their times. This chapter further outlines how social work is global, national and local, which calls for practitioners to understand, and challenge as necessary, the intersecting contexts of our work. The chapter will conclude with a case for exploring our 'new times' and mindful of dimensions of injustices and inequality and the unpredictability of contemporary worlds; we argue that there is value in social work reconnecting its theoretical and practical focus to one which is more sociological.

In Chapter 3 we take up the theme of imagination in practice as a fusion of what Mills conceptualises as a 'sociological imagination', together with creativity in disposition and practice. Stimulated by reading the ideas of creativity writers and social work writers such as Jane Adams,

Alice Salomon and Katherine van Wormer, key sociologists like Marx and Weber, and Charles Taylor, we elaborate on practical aspects of imagination in sociological social work. Chapter 4 extends this exploration using as a framework C. W. Mills' imaginative sensibilities (1970) to sketch imaginative 'habits' in social work practice. We focus on habits, a common approach in the creativity literature, and one Mills and Alice Salomon both advocated. We understand this way of working can be subsumed by other priorities when time is limited, social work demands are high and the organisational frameworks guiding practice focus attention in certain directions. As we say earlier, the contemporary social and political landscape brings with it heightened challenges to work for social justice and keep our critical openness. A sociological social work imagination, as a habit, can assist social workers to keep in their practice frame consideration and exploration of social worlds, social networks, processes and structures within which people are immersed and the social work imaginary expressed in international statements about the social work mission.

In Chapter 5 we tackle what is perhaps the most enduring question sociologists face: how much choice do individuals have in relation to their social settings? This chapter therefore explores the concept of choice or human agency as well as the theory of social structure. We explore social work values such as self-determination and autonomy alongside sociological concepts around selfhood and agency and argue for a deeper understanding of power, inequality and choice.

This leads us into Chapter 6, which explores the role of social relationships in social life. In understanding the somewhat shifting concept and experience of 'community', we place social relations as central to contemporary social work practice. Chapter 7 explores the concepts of time and space. These concepts help to shape the ways in which we describe and make sense of the social world. The notion of time is a neglected area of social work scholarship and yet it is realised through the day-to-day practices in which social workers engage. For example, there are various ways to conceptualise and theorise these concepts. We examine the role of the physical and conceptual concept of 'space'. Recent social work scholarship has contributed to this growing field. We explore recent sociological theorising in relation to historical and social meanings of space and apply these to the social work role.

Social work takes place in organisational contexts. In Chapter 8, we explore the role of the organisation – its rules, practices, policies, cultures and norms – and consider the particular organisationally informed practices that social work takes. Consistent with the theme of this book, understanding organisational life is assisted if we situate it within what happens in the organisational setting and the macro and historical context. Sociological perspectives can help us here. Gareth Morgan (2006), an organisational writer, has developed a typology of metaphors as ways to read and imagine organisational life, which he has condensed from an extensive review of the literature on organisations including the sociology of organisations. Using Morgan's approach and typology as a springboard, we illustrate how Morgan's process of 'metaphorisation' can be an aid to thinking sociologically about social work in organisational contexts.

One of the emerging areas of importance to social work is its empirical base. The need for social workers to argue for particular interventions in the current climate often requires evidence of the intervention's efficacy. Research-mindedness and social research are two concepts examined in Chapter 9. This chapter explores the nature of epistemology, the framing of research questions and applies sociological concepts to assist in framing social work as a research-informed social science. Chapter 10 concludes the book and draws together the main themes crucial to practising social work sociologically.

How to read this book

It is our hope that the reader can turn to which chapter appeals to them or resonates for them and be guided by their own interests. In this sense, it is not vital to read the text in a linear fashion, that is, from the first chapter to the final chapter. There are common elements to each chapter, for example, chapters explore issues central to social work and include an examination and application of social work and sociological theory in order to better understand the particular issues under consideration. Each chapter provides practical exercises and concludes with a section titled 'practising social work sociologically' in which we provide pointers of how social workers can use sociological theory in their practice.

We hope that this book is one of use to social work students, practitioners, and researchers alike. Our project is to bring sociological social work perspectives to contemporary practice. We draw on ideas from many sources in recognition that we are collective thinkers; our ideas are shaped by what we read and build upon and the insights that are generated. By reading this book, we hope you are opening up your thinking and imagination in what is an exciting and fulfilling way. Jane Addams reminds us about imagination, faith and courage:

What after all has maintained the human race on this old globe despite all the calamities of nature and all the tragic failings of mankind (sic), if not faith in new possibilities and courage to advocate them.

(Jane Addams)

2

Who Are We and What Do We Do?

Introduction

In this chapter we trace the contours of a sociological perspective and approach in social work, back to a time when indeed social work and sociology were new practices. We will explore this by looking through windows to the lives of three social workers. Each contributed to social work knowledge, and wrote about their social work practice and motivations. Jane Addams (1860–1935) from the United States and Alice Salomon (1872–1948) from Germany were active in pioneering social work. Both did so with an acute consciousness of social, economic and political contexts, displaying lively habits of imagination and intellect. These women lived and worked in the late nineteenth and early twentieth centuries, when sociology as a discipline was in its infancy (Giddens, 1989; Willis, 1999; MacLean and Williams, 2012). The third social worker we introduce is Clare Britton Winnicott (1906–1984), an influential English social worker whose casework during the Second World War was a response to the needs of displaced children. Clare Winnicott was influenced by, and in turn contributed to, psychoanalytical ideas and social work. She worked at a time in human history where the scale of events was to shift every conceivable underpinning in societies across the world.

Whilst of course each woman was her unique and distinctive person and social worker, from reading their writings we see shades of similarity between them which we draw out in this chapter. Between them their social work practice spanned a century – each lived and worked in different times, countries, cultures, settings – but there are discernible common aspects of their work that tell us both something about a social work for now and a social work for times ahead. They practised in ways that illustrate universal dimensions of social work but with anchors in the specificities of their time and place; in other words with roots in the social, cultural, economic and political contexts in which they lived.

Our reading of their work is that they shared a perspective on the interdependence of humans as social beings connected to one another; they shared an inexhaustible drive for understanding and change, and a perspective of society as a context and a focus of practice. They illustrate a reflexive capacity, humility and openness to be challenged, and to use what they learn to inform what they did. Each bumped up against sociological ideas and methods (Dunk-West and Verity, 2013, p. 10). Jane Addams was directly involved with the Chicago School of Sociology. Alice Salomon was a scholar and social worker in Germany when sociological thinking was in its infancy, and her sociological frame of reference is evident in her studies and writings. Clare Winnicott was influenced by psychoanalytic ideas in the post-Freudian tradition.

We are personally inspired by each of these social workers; they worked for social justice in times marked by the turning upside-down of previous social norms, and changing cultural and economic conditions. They passionately worked for change. As Jane Addams expresses it:

> *In the unceasing ebb and flow of justice and oppression we must all dig channels as best we may, that at the propitious moment somewhat of the swelling tide may be conducted to the barren places of life.*
>
> (Chapter 2, Loc 901, *Jane Addams: The Collected Works* ebook)

We are living in our own unique period of social and technological change that contemporary sociologists explain in various ways. Anthony Elliott expresses our times as marked by '... the multi-dimensional nature of social life in the late modern or postmodern age' (2003, p. 16). Zygmunt Bauman (1998) in a book entitled *Globalization: The Human Consequences* explores the differentiated impacts of globalization and 'time-space compression', themes that we pick up Chapter 7 when we discuss time and space. Ulrich Beck (1992) theorises about contemporary social worlds by employing the concept of 'risk society'. In this substantial work on risk he explores the interplay between a fracturing of established social and cultural practices, uncertainty and the acceleration of risk management cultures and practices. Beck reminds us to locate ourselves in relation to historical movements and developments and be able to identify social change and their impacts upon the ways in which we conceptualise who we are, what we think and what we do.

It is through understanding the social and historical interrelatedness of events and developments and the role of social work that we can better understand the forces which lead to inequality and injustice. In this chapter we outline the three social work pioneers. Our source material is both autobiographical writings by each of these three social workers, and academic commentaries and papers from the body of rich scholarship that explores their work, the references of which appear at the end of the book. Our purpose in sketching this picture of three social workers in their times, is to situate our own perspective on sociological social work as a larger historical concern, a view we share with other social work writers (e.g., van Wormer, 2002; Shaw, 2014), and which we explored in our earlier work (Dunk-West and Verity, 2013). We turn first to Jane Addams' scholarship and explore 'who she was and what she did'.

Jane Addams (1860–1935)

At the time Jane Addams was born in the United States in 1860, Western societies were undergoing social, political and technological changes that were unsettling practices of making things, working, relating and living; changes were occurring in the feel and form of community, what people did at work and what happened with their labouring, relations between humans and the natural world, and so on (Nisbet, 1966; Willis, 1999). Sociologists were engaged in explorations, looking for patterns and changes in experiences and social processes. As Willis (1999, pp. 3–4) writes, '*Each in their own way attempted to make sense of the changes that were occurring around them*'.

Early social workers were engaged in a not dissimilar project, but with the emphasis that defines social work, they were also responding to the human and collective needs that were ensuing from these profound social changes (Dunk-West and Verity, 2013). The motivation for their work variously was anchored in religious sentiments, political beliefs and a base in social justice. As we will see with Jane Addams and Alice Salomon, whom we come to next, change was a political, collective and personal project. It was also about engagement with ideas and they both demonstrate an insatiable search for understanding.

In this revolutionary context, Jane Addams was active as a social work pioneer; she was to be an inspiration to generations of social workers and activists and there is an extensive literature about her work. Whilst she is a woman who, in many respects, transcends categorisation we nonetheless describe her practice as activism, community development and social reformist practice. A feminist, and in 1931 the second women to win a Nobel Peace Prize, she was a co-founder of the international organisation *Women's International League for Peace and Freedom*, the American Sociological Society, and co-founder of Hull House in Chicago, the latter an organisation which had the goal of being a '… center for higher civic and social life; to institute and maintain educational and philanthropic enterprises, and to investigate and improve the conditions in the industrial districts of Chicago' (*Jane Addams: The Collected Works* ebook, Chapter 5, Loc 2411). Her work in Chicago was to be a life's project and the base for attention to local, national and international issues.

The Chicago that Jane Addams would have known was an industrial powerhouse; a magnet for economic capital and people from all over the world. Plummer describes how Chicago was the location of the early-twentieth-century Chicago School of Sociology, whose influence on sociological theory and approaches was to be considerable (Plummer, 1997). As we see in her autobiography, sociological and practical concerns preoccupied Jane Addams and her colleagues at Hull House. In reading her autobiographies we are struck by a woman who coupled thinking and action. MacLean and Williams suggest this dualism was not uncommon for the time, and they write:

> During the progressive era, as part of a larger Social Science Movement, practitioners under the label of sociology were teaching, investigating, writing, and advocating for social changes even as they built important programs for community services and social reforms.
>
> (2012, p. 238)

Jane Addams herself wrote extensively, soulfully and self-reflexively on all manner of topics recounting the activities of Hull House and exploring social and moral justice, social change and social work. She was a penetrating observer, thinker and analyst of social life and conditions. Her autobiographies are full of colourful and moving examples of the day-to-day happenings in the Hull House Settlement; they tell of the times as much as they do of her philosophy, heart and mind. Of Hull House she evocatively writes of conversations around the kitchen table, poetry recitals, a popular coffee house, day nursery, educational classes, health care, art and craft, recreation activities, a coal cooperative, men's club, provision of relief and information and '*drinking hot chocolate before an open fire*' (*Twenty Years at Hull House* ebook, Loc 1549, Chapter 7).

Local people were part of the Hull House community giving of their talents, sharing their ideas, catching and hatching their dreams with what Addams describes as 'infectious enthusiasm'. As she writes, Hull House was '*constantly filling and refilling with groups of people*' (*Jane Addams: The Collected Works* ebook, Chapter 7, Loc 3183) and attention to emergent needs was an active and constant process. However, there was more than this taking place. Residents of the House engaged in community development and lobbying about factory conditions, creation of employment schemes, supporting women who were victims of abuse and slavery, housing support and on it goes. We find the diversity, breadth and success of their collective efforts and care remarkable and inspirational. Consider some of the following activities that occurred at Hull House.

Hull House had a dedicated education programme: a Shakespeare club which ran for sixteen years, lectures, a Plato club, and English classes for newly arrived immigrants. There were social debates about sociological and political issues and this resonated with the wider spirit of political debate which was a hallmark of these times. One medium for this dialogue was a Social Science Club, set up at about the same time the University of Chicago commenced the first sociology department in the United States. Jane Addams recalls the club '*convinced the residents that no one so poignantly realizes the failures in the social structure as the man [sic] at the bottom, who has been most directly in contact with those failures and has suffered most*' (*Jane Addams: The Collected Works* ebook, Chapter 9, Loc 3895–3912). Enthusiasm for debate and dialogue are noted by Jane Addams in her autobiography:

> 'The Working People's Social Science Club' as organised at Hull House in the spring of 1890 by an English working man, and for seven years it held a weekly meeting. At eight o'clock every Wednesday night the secretary called to over from forty to one hundred people; a speaker was introduced who was allowed to talk until nine o'clock; his subject was then thrown open to discussion and a lively debate ensued until ten o'clock, at which hour the meeting was adjourned ... the enthusiasm for this club seldom lagged.
>
> (*Jane Addams: The Collected Works* ebook, Chapter 9, Loc 3829)

Residents were themselves social analysts undertaking local research using scientific methods of inquiry; as we note earlier, studies were about the food values of local communities, sweatshop conditions, neighbourhood conditions, poverty, garbage and sanitation, working hours. Investigations were thorough and driven by wanting to change something, whether this be changes to the law, public understanding, urban practices or human behaviours. The focus on the broader macro conditions of a society and the immediate individual concerns is apparent in the following extract, where Jane Addams is explicit about the need to address and close inequality gaps, as well as respond to individual circumstances:

> The Settlement then, is an experimental effort to aid in the solution of the social and industrial problems which are engendered by the modern conditions of life in a great city. It insists that these problems are not confined to any one portion of a city. It is an attempt to relieve, at the same time, the overaccumulation at one end of society and the destitution at the other; but it assumes that this overaccumulation and destitution is most sorely felt in the things that pertain to social and educational privileges.
>
> (*Jane Addams: The Collected Works* ebook, Chapter 6, Loc 2730)

In recent times there has been a renewed focus on practitioner research. We have clear examples of this approach in the goings on at Hull House.

Exercise

Jane Addams' work reflected an emphasis on both the broader macro conditions of a society and the immediate individual and neighbourhood community concerns.

➢ Reflect on what this approach means for social work practice in general.

➢ How might you actively maintain this dual focus throughout your work?

Summary

In summary, Jane Addams' life work as a community development social worker, activist, reformer and sociologist speaks directly about a practical sociologically informed social work. In reading her autobiographies it seems there was a seamless connection between her values, vision and spirit of curiosity about why things are as they are; between these attributes and practical techniques for systematic action research, and creative and dogged efforts to improve social conditions. She did not stand still in her thinking and quest to understand and act from that understanding. Scientific research and sociological thinking were part of her practice. The residents of the Hull House community and surrounds were at the heart of this action; it was their 'infectious enthusiasm' at work. In awarding Jane Addams the Noble Peace Prize, the Committee notes, *'From this social work, often carried on among people of different nationalities, it was for her only a natural step to the cause of peace'* (Koht, 1931). We now move on to consider the work of Alice Salomon.

Alice Salomon (1872–1948)

At about the same time as Jane Addams was working in North America, across the Atlantic Alice Salomon was active in activism, social reform, intellectual and social work educational pursuits. She established one of the first social work schools in Europe (Wieler, 1988, p. 166) and her extraordinary work lives on in the Alice Salomon University located in Berlin. The values of Alice Salomon, which we expand upon later in this chapter, are evident in the University's website welcome message:

'Refugees and Newcomers: Welcome to our University' (https://www.ash-berlin.eu/en/). She lived and worked through periods of war, and as she writes, was 'influenced by what it bred' (2004, p. 105).

When Jane Addams was twelve years old, Alice Salomon was born in Berlin into a 'middle class Jewish family' (Lees, 2004, p. 1; Wieler, 1988). Like Jane Addams, throughout her adult life she was active in the women's movement, peace activism, and combined practical work, intellectual pursuits and research. She was a researcher and scholar having undertaken her PhD on a study entitled 'The Causes of Unequal Payment for Men's and Women's Work' (Wieler, 1988, p. 165). Lees (2004, p. viiii) states Alice Salomon '… published more than two dozen books and well over four hundred articles between 1895 and 1937', a quite staggering output. Wieler (1988) describes how much of this was destroyed by the Nazis.

Alice Salomon, in her autobiography *Character Is Destiny*, describes her early life influencers and in the following extract she captivatingly conveys her will and habits to seek change and justice. Note her use of the phrase 'habitual attitude' in the first sentence of this extract:

> 'Something has to be done about it,' became a habitual attitude with me, not only when I met with a human problem but when a flower in the school garden looked sickly. My colleagues used to tease me for it. But to this day I say that something has to be done about the troubles of the world, and I have tried throughout my life to do at least a little of what needed doing.
>
> (2004, p. 20)

Her entry into social work was through engagement with a charitable organisation where she undertook both practical work with individuals and families. In the following citation from her autobiography, note the reference to education in sociology, Jane Addams' work in Chicago and the need for creativity:

> I also attended lecture courses on sociology and civics arranged by our organization. It was one of the first attempts to devise some theoretical preparation for social work. All this began in the year 1893, when Jane Addams moved into Hull House in Chicago and Lillian Wald in New York went to live on Henry Street to nurse her neighbors. English men and women had preceded us with similar efforts, but we knew nothing of each other. Social work had no history, no rules, no models. It needed creative personalities. It was pioneering and opened a new field.
>
> (2004, p. 25)

Alice Salomon's commitment to creatively explore and understand underlying causes of social issues, and what could be done to secure justice and peace, are defining and motivating characteristics of her work.

Like Addams she was part of a movement that worked with the 'poor'. She writes 'Our League for Social Work came into existence through the efforts of a group of progressive people. ... It was an equivalent of the Anglo-Saxon settlement movement' (2004, p. 27). It is not surprising then that she was to come under the surveillance and persecution of the Nazi regime, and in the late 1930s to be expelled from Germany, to live the final years of her life in New York. Wieler, who has written about Alice Salomon's life and work, puts it thus:

> Her work on behalf of peace and disarmament antithetical to the country's military aspirations. Her struggle for women's rights conflicted with the Party's position respecting the proper role of women. Her status as an intellectual gave her dangerous authority and high visibility. And perhaps worst of all was her position in social work and social work education.
>
> (Wieler, 1988, p. 168)

Aside from a unity of the practical and intellectual, her international perspective is also instructive. Alice Salomon had a particular international interest and sensibility which was to permeate her work (Fuestal, ud). Wieler (1988) attributes this to her upbringing and familiarity with her family's business affairs outside of Germany. This internationalism was manifest in her scholarly work, teaching and her collaborations to establish a global social work network, first known as the International Committee on Schools of Social Work (ICSSW). An acute awareness and interest in international dimensions of social and economic conditions, we can call it an international perspective, was intrinsic to the thinking of social workers like Alice and her colleague Jane Addams; they were part of a global network, and acted from this sensibility. It is also reflected in Alice Salomon's research, which was comparative across cultures, geography and socio-economic contexts. We might think of globalisation as a recent phenomenon but these women's lives show that an international perspective is not new in social work, a point made by van Wormer (2002) in her work on social work imagination. We return to this theme as it has direct relevance to the sociological social work approach we argue is needed in these contemporary times.

In reading about Alice Salomon's work and extracts from her autobiography we are struck by her penetrating thinking on the significance of social work and her insights into the knowledge base required for supporting this work. Not only was she prolific, as we state earlier, she explored and wrote on all matters under the sun in what can only be called a holistic and integrative way; she wrote about society, economics, women and care and a range of other sociological topics. Her ideas on labouring, exploitation and consumer responsibility are early traces of what is now described as corporate social responsibility. A paper written by Alice Salomon which resonates with the perspective we discuss in this book is entitled 'Education of Social Work: A Sociological Interpretation Based on an International Survey' (1937). Fuestal has read across Salomon's works and she notes the following:

> These [texts] conjure an impression of someone who appears to have collected examples by keeping an eye on whatever crossed her path – a snippet from someone's lecture, conversations at a congress, news from a personal contact, a discourse, impressions and material from a trip – but each time, the illustration attains special significance.

> (ud, p. 7)

Exercise

Alice Salomon used the phrase 'habitual attitudes' to refer to her approach when 'seeing something was not right' of 'doing something about it'.

➤ What comes to your mind when you think about these words 'habitual attitudes'?

➤ What would you say is one of your 'habitual attitudes' and how do you use this in your own social work?

Summary

In summary, from our reading of Alice Salomon's work we can assemble some key parts of a scaffolding for a sociological social work practice. She talks about the need for creativity, 'habitual attitudes', integrative thinking, an international sensibility and a praxis linking thinking and action. In Chapter 3, and following Alice Salomon's lead, we will explore in more detail habits of imagination and place them as an intrinsic aspect of sociological social work practice. Wieler (1988, p. 171) in concluding a paper about Alice Salomon notes that Alice 'held that "the most funda-mental law in human relations is the law of interdependence". It is a law by which she lived'. This concept of inter-dependence, of humans linked pro-foundly with each other, links between the social and the personal, the inner world and the outer world, and of the people across the planet, is a segue into the work of another social worker, Clare Britton Winnicott, who articulated a similar value of 'the common humanity that binds us and our clients together' (2004, Chapter 9, Loc 4271). We now turn to a brief overview of Clare Winnicott's social work and contributions to knowl-edge before returning to our theme of sociological social work practice.

Clare Britton Winnicott (1906–1984)

Born in 1906, the year that Alice Salomon obtained her PhD, Clare Winnicott was a casework social worker and psychoanalyst, and, similarly to our other social workers, she was an educator, intellectual, writer and social work trail blazer. She was to become a pioneer in university level education of social workers working with children, before generic social work courses (Kanter, 2004). Unlike our other social workers Clare had direct casework practice experience and many of her intellectual developments were focused on child and family case work practice and mental health social work (Holmes, 2004). Over the course of her career she worked in public sector positions, as an educator at the London School of Economics and as a psychoanalyst.

We include her as one of social work's pioneers for similar reasons to Jane Addams and Alice Salomon: her focus on the use of good scientific method, theory in practice, and a curious disposition. Like our other social work pioneers, Clare Winnicott too wrote extensively and widely, on subject matters such as empathy, authenticity, social work insight and self-awareness, supervision, communication and engagement with children (Kanter, 2004). It might seem on the face of it that psychoanalytical thinking is a stranger to sociological thinking, but a distinctive aspect of Clare's work was her intense concern with social context, what Holmes calls her focus on 'the *whole picture*' (Holmes, Loc 291 of 5947, 2004).

Clare Winnicott's motivation for social work was a fusion of her early life experiences and the values that had roots in her family upbringing and social context. An insight into this motivation is seen in the following extract from a 1980 interview by Alan Cohen:

A.C. How did you come into social work, Mrs. Winnicott?

C.W. How did I come into it? I suppose through a friend of the family. And in a way my family had always been interested in social work. My father had run a club for unemployed people, my grandfather had taken quite a big part in the social situation where he lived. I think it was in the family.

A.C. When was it you first came into social work? Was it during the war or before the war?

C.W. Before the war. Before the war I went and worked in YWCA clubs simply because a friend of my mother's was in charge of a YWCA centre and she invited me to go and work in the centre. And I did. Then I went to the LSE [1] afterwards to take social science. (Cohen, 2013 p.2)

A significant period was her work in Oxfordshire with evacuated and orphaned children during the Second World War years. It was while here that she met Donald Winnicott, paediatrician and psychoanalyst, whom she was later to marry (Kanter, 2004). Donald Winnicott is a significant figure in child development literature for his conceptualistion of an 'intermediate space' between people's inner and outer worlds, and, for example, understandings about the role of 'transitional objects' like dollies, teddy bears or blankets, which mediate between self-discovery and stepping away from the caregiver and coming back to safe bases (Kanter, 1996). Joel Kanter (2004), editor of Clare Winnicott's collected writings, notes her contributions to Donald's conceptual work and his theories about effective practice with children and families. He suggests she was also 'down to earth' and made concepts understandable and practically relevant and gives an example where she renamed Donald's concept of 'transitional objects' to be instead a 'first treasured possession' (2004, Preface, Loc 758 of 5947).

We describe earlier that both Jane Addams and Alice Salomon were deeply conscious and reflexive about their values and the need to see individuals in their societal context. From her standpoint as a caseworker with children and families Clare similarly illustrates this sensibility. Holmes (2004, Loc 270 of 5947) writes that Clare Winnicott held the '... view of the psyche and of social life was essentially dynamic in that she saw both as a resultant of a balance of forces'. In her own words, she expresses this interplay as follows:

> We could easily get bogged down in the detail of the family dynamics of the individual, and lose sight of the structure. I feel so strongly that the two things have to go together. We have to be altering the structure to meet the individual, and helping the individual within the structure. I think you can't ever take your hand off either of these things. It's tremendously important and it always has been to me, to see the context in which I'm working.
>
> (Cohen, 2013, p. 19)

The relational dynamic of agency and structure, or links between the 'macro' and the 'micro', is an important dimension in social work and one we pick up more comprehensively in later chapters. Jane Addams writes her values were 'not philanthropy nor benevolence, but a thing fuller and wider than either of these' (Loc 2601, ebook), which she articulates as a project based on a common humanity or good:

> ... it is difficult to see how the notion of a higher civic life can be fostered save through common intercourse; ... that the good we secure for ourselves is precarious and uncertain, is floating in mid-air, until it is secured for all of us and incorporated into our common life.
>
> (Chapter 6, Loc 2487, ebook)

Clare Winnicott expresses something similar in writing:

> In my view it is only if we can, as social workers, accept within ourselves the common humanity that binds us and our clients together, that we shall be able to empathise with them, and understand their vulnerability because we too, are vulnerable. Perhaps the most valuable gift that we bring to work with children is our own capacity to remain vulnerable, while accepting our professional discipline and role.
>
> (2004, Chapter 9, Loc 4270)

Summary

In summary, from our reading of Clare Winnicott's work, both commentaries from her biographers and what she herself wrote, we can draw out some themes to take forward in our exploration of social work and sociological thinking and practice. Clare Winnicott displays a keen and wise focus on empathy and imagination and seeing the interplay of lived experience and context. Her strong values and practical ways of communicating and engaging are striking. Holmes calls this the fusion of '... her unique blend of common sense and psychoanalytic insight' (2004, Loc 270 of 5947). We will return to the idea of imagination as empathy in the next chapter.

Exercise

Clare Winnicott's work brings home the importance of connecting the 'micro' and the 'macro' in social work and the need to see individuals in their societal context.

Spend some time thinking about how this perspective is important in social work with individuals.

Practice in a global world

What does this brief excursion into the lives of three social workers tell us about who and what we are, and the contours of a sociological perspective and approach in social work? Jane Addams, Clare Winnicott and Alice Salomon each were social workers of conviction and commitment to social work values, whose work was a response to the vicissitudes of their times. This focus on social work and society is part of the social work history and tradition – what Jane Addams called a 'channel dug'. They name sensibilities and practices we believe are as much needed now as they were in the times in which they lived. They lived and worked in times of social change and actively worked to understand these changes and how to best support human beings in their socially shaped lives. Clare Winnicott did this in her work with children and families. Jane Addams did this in supporting the development of spaces for care, community and justice. Alice Salomon did this in drawing attention to exploitation and the need for social justice, for example in her study of labour and working conditions. Looking through contemporary eyes we might name their social work practice differently, but they share what sociologists Bauman and May call the critical processes 'to *render manifest what is latent*' (2001, p. 177) and to develop theoretical and practice approaches based on this knowledge.

We are all aware, in different ways, how we are living and being social workers in another time of change and uncertainty. Just take the day-to-day impacts and implications of digital technology. We see these impacts in how economies and markets work, the global and local and regional emergent forms of communication, possibilities that are opening up for identity and self-making, and for our very conceptions and experiences of time and space. The sociologist Manual Castells (1996), over twenty years ago, coined the phrase a 'network society' to describe a world criss-crossed by the spinning of nets of connectivity, the weavers of which are digital technology, time/space compression and processes of globalisation. These nets of connectivity are changing and developing rapidly. Think about technological developments which seem to change on a weekly basis as new devices and apps emerge and the globalising influences on our societal institutions, but also the resistance to these trends with nationalist and localisation movements. The rapidity of these technological advances is unprecedented and the speed at which these developments have taken place has altered time itself (Lash), as we explore in the chapter on space and time.

Technology is also changing the nature of work. Martin Ford (2015) in a book *The Rise of Robots-Technology and the Threat of a Jobless Future* investigates how machines are now becoming the labourers and increasingly, that jobs as we have known them in the past have, as he states, 'vaporised'. What will this development mean for human life and social care and social work into the future? Ford writes:

> We are, in all likelihood, at the leading edge of an explosive wave of innovation that will ultimately produce robots geared toward nearly every conceivable commercial, industrial and consumer task.
>
> (2015, p. 6)

Exercise

If we think about the jobs that are available now, compared with those from only one or two generations ago, we can see many shifts. Take a moment to think about relatives from one generation ago and think about the family labour.

What kind of work was available to those relatives and what skills were required? Was one income enough to support a family?

What supports were in place for those people not in paid labour? What about two generations ago? Your grandparents' parents? What about your situation?

Inequality within countries and between the northern and southern hemispheres is growing. Sir Michael Marmot presented the 2016 Australian Boyer Lectures at which he made a sobering statistical comparison that underscores the unequal distribution of capital resources across the planet. He said:

> What do Tanzania, Paraguay, Latvia and the top 25 earning hedge fund managers in the US have in common? The answer is that the 48 million people of Tanzania, the 7 million people of Paraguay, the 2 million people of Latvia and the top 25 hedge fund managers each have an annual income of between \$21 and \$28 billion US dollars.
>
> (Marmot, 2016)

Think of the movement of people across the world and the suffering being experienced by so many because of war and displacement, for example in Syria. The United Nation's Refugee Agency continues to report record high levels of people being displaced across the globe (UNHCR, 2014). What does this say about our 'common life' to use Jane Addams' phrase? In 2016, 51 per cent of displaced people are children (UNHCR, 2016). What might Clare Winnicott have made of this state of affairs?

Think of what social work also brings into the frame about who we are and what we do: strengths and assets, a belief in people and what is done individually and collectively with and for each other. Jane Addams' autobiographies of life in Hull House in Chicago are bursting with examples of solidarity, kindness and care. Think of loving relationships, community development, care and work for social justice and peace that takes place every minute of the day all over the globe. We see that with responses to events such as terrorist attacks, the solidarity within communities after disasters, in campaigns and rallies and other actions that tell about a different narrative.

Conclusions

But what is ahead and where should social work be in thinking and practice in this changing world? This we believe is a question that can only be answered by a thoughtful practice where ideas and investigation of the dynamic social world come together in what we do as social workers. This, we suggest, is who we are and what we do. We hope in this book that we are able to make a contribution to the more recent groundswell joining or re-joining sociology and social work (e.g., MacLean and Williams, 2012; Shaw, 2014) and to a tide-turning in ideas and practices that we see taking place.

Practising social work sociologically

From a brief look at the lives of three pioneering social workers we observe a spirit of practising social work 'sociologically'. In this chapter we have explored the ways in which thinking about other nations, and social and cultural change impact on individual experiences. Jane Addams, Alice Salomon and Clare Winnicott convey a commitment to the active role that social workers play in challenging and changing social conditions and addressing inequalities. These pioneers contribute the following aspects of a sociological social work:

➤ Empathy and identification of our common humanity.

➤ Social work practice based in 'common intercourse', humility and knowing ourselves well.

➤ International sensibilities in a global world which stretch our thinking about the 'social' and our local context.

➤ Creative enquiry and learning as part of understanding underlying structural patterns, what we might take for granted, and what might be done.

➤ Keeping critical deep thinking and action together.

➤ Action that contributes to change at a societal level and change at the community, family and individual level.

➤ 'Habitual attitudes' and practices.

3

Imagination in Practising Social Work Sociologically

Introduction

When you think of the word 'imagination', what comes to mind? You might associate it with a personal characteristic such as being curious or creative; perhaps you think in the abstract about images, or it is an image itself that comes to mind. Maybe you associate imagination with creativity and the arts. We also often associate the use of imagination in relation to children. If you have been around pre-school- and primary-school-aged children, for example, you would see imagination in use through play. The ways in which children take on roles of others – such as police person, super hero, doctor – requires the suspension of concrete reality through the application of imagination which creates imaginary worlds, characters and events.

Throughout this book runs a thread of the value of sociological ideas to understanding and appreciating possibilities in a transforming world. How do we imagine and understand this transformation? As social workers, how do we see the possibilities for the realisation of core values of social justice and human rights, which are at the heart of social work? (Dunk-West and Verity, 2013). This is where we believe an explicit attention to imagination comes into play, to support a move towards thinking about these questions, not just in the abstract but in a practical and applied sense. This is an exercise of imagination where sociological theories can inform our thoughts and interpretations, where alternative thinking can emerge, out of which new ways of action can come to be.

However, attention to imagination in social work and social care can be played down within a dominant twenty-first-century managerialist frame of reference (Froggett, 2002; Jackson and Burgess, 2005). In her book called 'Love, Hate and Welfare', Lynn Froggett makes the point that:

> Managerialism allows people to distance themselves from the emotional impact of their work, watch their backs, and mind their careers. However, the

costs in terms of lost creativity, or simply ability to establish a realistic relation to reality, are immeasurable.

(2002, p. 81)

In 2002, Katherine van Wormer wrote a paper entitled 'Our Social Work Imagination: How Social Work Has Not Abandoned Its Mission' in which she compellingly sketches her argument that imagination and social work go hand in hand. Ferguson's work (2011), which is based on tracing the practices of social workers in child protection, points to the need to better understand the micro, creative and emotional domains of this kind of work. What we see from this kind of scholarship is an argument for social work to be seen as both a social science as well as an art. In the context of scientific rationality, social work needs to maintain and appreciate the creative practices of both clients and social workers.

Our starting point in this chapter is acknowledgement of a well-trodden road that places imagination not only as a crucial aspect of social work, but also that there are constraints on how we might express imagination. Here we synthesise and build on ideas in the social work literature to advance our case for imagination in practising social work sociologically (i.e., Addams, ud; Lee, 1994; Winnicott, 1996; Fook, 1999; van Wormer, 2002; Froggett, 2002; Salomon, 2004; Jackson and Burgess, 2005). We outline three perspectives on imagination: empathy as an aspect of imagination; Charles Taylor's idea about a social imaginary; and C. Wright Mills' 'sociological imagination'.

Imagination

Imagination takes us outside our rational existence. When we read a fictional work or watch a film, we take ourselves outside our daily existence and enter into a suspended state of disbelief where we enter a different time and space (Monaco, 2000). This act requires imagination: the 'ability to think outside ourselves'. Imagination is also the capacity to dream and create a possible in one's mind. The nineteenth-century poet Emily Dickinson writes:

The Gleam of an heroic act,
Such strange illumination-
The Possible's slow fuse is lit
By the Imagination!

Her lines 'the Possible's slow fuse is lit / By the imagination' evoke an image of the power of the imagination in creating the possible, the energy released at the end of the fuse. Emily Dickinson's image captures some of the themes we will explore. Firstly, the link between imagination and the 'possible' has relevance to social work, which, in its application, is essentially about seeking out and co-creating a 'possible', often in situations in which this might not feel at all likely. What does 'possibility' look like? The possibility of being seen for who we are and treated accordingly; people living free from intimidating and violent relationships; the possibility of not living in poverty, having meaningful employment; the possibility of being respected and loved; the possibility of having a hoped-for future: these are all examples of possibility in action. Depending on ideological differences we will have varying imaginations about how these possibilities are attained.

Eva Hoff, in her work on play and creativity, defines imagination as follows:

> Imagination can be defined as involving cognitive processes in which memories, former experience and images are combined into new constructions.
>
> (2003, p. 405)

However, imagination is more than a characteristic of an individual; it is this, but it is what Appadurai describes as a social and cultural practice and process (Appadurai, 1996). The stuff of imagination draws from social and cultural worlds, giving us a library of images. Think about the role of literature and the arts in inspiring what we think about and what we learn as we go through life. The philosopher Martha Nussbaum (1997) in her work on literature and morality gives an example of how imagination is embedded in socio-cultural practices. She writes:

> When a child and a parent begin to tell stories together, the child is acquiring essential moral capacities. Even a simple nursery rhyme such as 'Twinkle, twinkle, little star, how I wonder what you are' leads children to feel wonder – a sense of mystery that mingles curiosity with awe.
>
> (1997, p. 89)

Poets such as William Blake use this sense of wonder to associate childhood with purity, nature and the antithesis of reason. This wonder, experienced by both a child hearing a story and parent as storyteller, as Nussbaum explains, has a role in human social development. Child education curricula with the emphasis on creativity and imaginative play attest to this.

Imagination is one of those concepts that can be explored differently, and we see this in the rather large body of knowledge about imagination:

Exercise

When you think of the word 'imagination' what comes to mind?

What supports your imagination?

How do you use imagination in your social work practice?

How has your imagination changed over time?

---

psychology (e.g., exploring imagination as a psychosocial process); education (e.g., in creative learning and human development); creative disciplines (e.g., imagination in poetry, film, literature, sound and various digital mediums); philosophy and theology (e.g., what is the mysterious?); and knowledge also in disciplines that include management, and engineering.

Perhaps something from all these rich traditions is embodied in the life of Leonardo da Vinci, who as writer, architect, artist, inventor and scientist has long been associated with living the quintessential imaginative existence (Gelb, 1998). Edward de Bono's work is another example and his exposition on lateral thinking, the practice of using coloured thinking hats and creativity has been hugely influential across the world (1973). Harnessing imagination and creativity is a significant feature of business corporate practices. We only have to see how much Google spend on research and development ($8 billion or 13.2% of their revenue in the year 2013[1]) to gain a sense of how serious imaginative innovation that results in development of new ideas is to their company objectives. Google are not unusual here. Market share and sustainable profits are key drivers in the pursuit of discoveries and new ideas and have been for centuries.

Whilst there are therefore numerous ways that imagination is defined, we refer to imagination and imaginative practices in social work practice in two ways. At one level, imagination is about cognitive processes, or the workings of the 'mind's eye' where pictures and ideas are formed and used to produce something 'new or anew' (Gelb, 1998; Thomas, 1999). As van Wormer (2002) writes, this imagination can manifest in numerous ways in social work: in 'originality' and 'resourcefulness', how we use insights that change our perceptions, and most importantly, what we actually do think about. Jackson and Burgess (2005, p. 5) also hone in on

---

[1] Source: *Fortune Magazine*: http://fortune.com/2014/11/17/top-10-research-development/

these qualities in their exploration of creativity in social work, and what they describe as the '... imagination and creativity to support this inventiveness'. It is also expressed in how we structure time to connect to a creative spirit, both our own inner creative capacities and how we support this capacity for others (van Wormer, 2002; Froggett, 2002; Jackson and Burgess, 2005). This creative expression might be seen in what we say and do, and also could be through mediums that can allow access to and expression of emotions and thoughts.

But we are also using this term to refer to C. Wright Mills' (1970) 'Sociological Imagination'; what he terms as the 'deftness' to make conceptual connections that assist us to see patterns in the operations of social structures, power relations and human lives in a given society and time period. This is the second way we define imagination, which is how we use our 'mind's eye' to see outside of and beyond the individual and the 'taken for granted' (Bauman and May, 2001) to the dynamics and processes of the social worlds in which we live, and their implications. Bauman and May call this thinking 'sociologically'. Sociological understandings are generated in the exercise of such an imagination, which can support keeping a social context alive in our work with individuals, groups, communities and in advocacy and influencing public policy.

The imaginative habits we talk about are then at two points on the same plane: a habit of imagination as the warp and weft of creative insight and action, together with a way to see what can be taken for granted (Bauman and May, 2001, p. 177). These two points are both in the same line of vision and so we can connect them, but the second habit is just that much further on, and so we need to be more determined to reach for it. A habit of imagination is an approach to assist the social worker in navigating the world of the service or agency, itself located in wider social structures and to steer through the constraints within the agency that limit the social work role and creativity. For example, imagination can be used to see how social work in many parts of the world is moulded by hegemonic neo-liberal policies. This might manifest in individualised practice, and experiences of working within tight eligibility criteria and competitive service provision. Consistent with the approach taken in this book, we present practical ways that this sort of imagination can be nurtured as a habit of effective practice. This is the focus of Chapter 4.

Empathy and imagination

Empathy is a key requirement for social workers. For social workers to contribute to the creation of a possible that means something to the people with whom we work requires us to be mindful of people's presents, pasts and futures, and cognisant of the social structures that give meaning, context and futures. This calls upon us to respect people's subjectivity and agency, and place this in a temporal and social-cultural context. We ourselves are not absent from the picture and need to also understand ourselves as agents in these imaginative processes. Katherine van Wormer (2002) is a social work academic who has written compellingly about a social work imagination as an intrinsic aspect of our work. She further makes the point, which we share and is evident in other work (i.e., Froggett, 2002; Jackson and Burgess, 2005), that social work practice abounds with examples of imagination and creativity. Van Wormer defines a social work imagination as '... *that combination of empathy, suspension of disbelief, insight and resourcefulness that makes for exceptional social work practice*' (2002, p. 32). She puts empathy first, and this takes us to the arguably defining aspect of social work, which is the imaginative and emotional ability for attunement with another, or with groups of people.

There are many examples in the social work literature that link imagination and empathy. Let's trace this theme across time. Clare Winnicott, whom we introduced in Chapter 2, writes about imagination in the following way:

> The freedom that social workers have to use themselves in these situations will depend on each one's capacity to identify with others and to imaginatively encompass the experience of their clients in any given situation.
>
>   (2004, Chapter 9, Loc 4110 of 5947)

Compton and Galaway writing in the 1970s link empathy and imagination for social work and outline the importance of imagination to better understand the people with whom we work:

> In learning to be empathetic, workers have to develop the capacity for imaginative consideration of others and to give up any fixed mental image that may lead one to change reality to fit any preconceived expectation.
>
>   (Compton and Galaway, 1979, p. 176)

Jackson and Burgess note a similar point in their work on creativity and social work. They argue that imagination and empathy help us to 'hold off' our own experiences and perceptions so that we can see the world from our client's perspective:

> Creativity within the initial problem working process is bound up with thoughtful and empathetic communication and enquiry aimed at facilitating the construction of a narrative that combines the client's story with the

clinician's evaluative commentary from which hypotheses are created and tested, and ultimately judgements made.

(2005, p. 7)

When we have situations all around the world where people are viewed and acted upon as the 'other', whether on the basis of their religion, abilities, culture, race and ethnicity, age and preferences in how they wish to love and live, it is urgent that there is an active use of empathy with social justice (Nussbaum, 1997). We have world leaders who are demonstrating and mobilising these prejudices in calls to build walls to keep people out, and to turn back asylum seekers arriving in boats despite deaths on the seas and the perilous situations in the places from which they come. The vitriol expressed by online trolls is another example, together with cyberbullying and harassment in school yards and workplaces. We see on our televisions daily the poverty and hardship faced by many people across the world, but what do we do. Empathy requires an ability to imagine being in someone else's shoes and accordingly relate to what someone else is recounting as their experiences, but, as King writes, 'simultaneously be open to the meanings ascribed by the client [*sic*] and other potentially healing alternatives and explanations' (2011, p. 685).

It is common for frameworks defining social work empathy to include interacting components of the 'affective', 'cognitive', and 'behavioural' (Compton and Galaway, 1979; Gerdes and Segal, 2009; King, 2011). Gerdes and Segal, for example, note the importance of stitching empathic understanding together with social work values as the essential material of our social work practice. They write: 'As social workers, to be empathic is to experience the affect, process it, and then take appropriate, effective, empathy-driven action. The empathic actions we take can impact individuals, groups, communities and even society' (2009, p. 122). Empathy is often expressed as the quality to 'make the imaginative leap into the life of the other' and we see this in the work of Nussbaum and others (Nussbaum, 1997; Krznaric, 2008). There could not be a more pressing time to engage our empathic selves in what Nussbaum calls the task of 'cultivating humanity'.

Imagining social objectives

In addition to the above aspects of imagination, as social workers we imagine social objectives and principles that inform our social work practice. These social imaginings are a framework of abstract concepts and visions, and give social workers a shared value orientation; values and ideals give us a collective direction or aim as a guide to individual and collective practice. Reproduced below is the International Federation of Social Work's description of social work, which is a succinct narrative of the ambition of the social work mission.

Global Definition of the Social Work Profession

'Social work is a practice-based profession and an academic discipline that promotes social change and development, social cohesion, and the empowerment and libera-tion of people. Principles of social justice, human rights, collective responsibility and respect for diversities are central to social work. Underpinned by theories of social work, social sciences, humanities and indigenous knowledge, social work engages people and structures to address life challenges and enhance wellbeing. The above definition may be amplified at national and/or regional levels.' (2014, IFSW website, http://ifsw.org/policies/definition-of-social-work/)

Not only is the IFSW's description of social work an exercise in imagi-nation by its social work writers, as we note earlier, but it is an interweav-ing of social objectives. These social imaginings include ideals about 'social change', 'social justice', 'social cohesion', and 'empowerment' and 'liberation' and are based in future-oriented visions or mental maps about how our world and people's individual and collective lives could be. It is a collective vision or what Appadurai (1996, p. 31) calls 'imagination as a social practice'.

But what is it we imagine? In contemplating the IFSW social work objectives, we use our imaginations to interpret what these concepts might mean, drawing on our own values and ideology, experiences and thoughts, and the breadth of ideas we are exposed to through thinking, reading and talking. We also get the sense of these imaginations from somewhere, from our understandings of the dynamics and structures of our wider society. Before we continue with a discussion of the IFSW social objectives, we introduce a perspective on the social imaginary.

Charles Taylor is a philosopher who has set out his perspective on the notion of a social imaginary in the context of exploring the devel-opment of a 'moral order of modern societies'. A particular focus in his work are the processes by which we collectively imagine or conjure up in a social 'mind' the dynamics of the social space or societies in which we live, the moral orders and the implicit rules by which we socially interact, and how such processes become embedded and reproduced in societies. He talks about this social imaginary as 'an enabler' which makes action possible, and which is part of the process by which change happens. In his own words, he states:

> I am thinking, rather, of the ways people imagine their social existence, how they fit together with others, how things go on between them and their fellows, the expectations that are normally met, and the deeper normative notions and images that underlie these expectations.
>
> (Taylor, 2004, p. 23)

He describes that a sense of this social imaginary can be just that, a common sense or intuitive knowledge. Again, in his own words:

> ... for most of human history, and for most of social life, we function through the grasp we have on the common repertory, without benefit of theoretical overview. Humans operated with a social imaginary, well before they ever got into the business of theorizing about themselves.
>
> (Taylor, 2004, p. 26)

Across his work (2004) Taylor outlines in detail what he sees to be the key features of social life in the secular modern Western social imaginary. In contrast to previous historical periods where religious institutions and the upper classes and nobility set the moral way or order, the modern social imaginary is characterised by what Taylor sets out as key features of the '... economy, public sphere, and a polity ruled by the people' and a 'notion of human rights'. He explains the presence of these features represent a shift from 'vertical or hierarchal order to horizontal processes' across Western societies. Of relevance here is the framing of a collective process of imagining, and the role of the common space in enabling this imagination. The ideals of theorists play a role in sparking the imagination of the collective (Taylor, 2004).

In our collective work as social workers we operate with a social imaginary. The civil society group the IFSW express these social objectives as a beacon; there is a call for a proactive dimension to change at the level of people's individual, family or community lives, and change in the wider policies, structures and norms of the various societies across the world. This requires change to rectify what is now unjust, disempowering and oppressive. The concept of social justice, to which social work is committed, enables social workers to imagine the re-organisation of power relations in order to achieve a better world. The use of the imagination to see the possible is required to work toward this goal, but it also implies that we see beyond individual circumstances and locate people's experiences in the broader social, cultural, political and historical context. We also come together in civil society, through organisations such as social work associations which enable us to collectively reinforce our understandings and imaginations of these values and objectives.

Exercise

Think about empowerment, which is a fundamental aspect of social work. Empowerment is the understanding of inequality and the ways in which people can address inequality through better access to services, education or knowledge, for example.

➢ How do you know what you know about empowerment?

➢ What are the mental pictures and ideas in your 'mind's eye' about empowerment? How do you draw on memories and feelings when you have experienced empowerment or seen it displayed, or when you have seen or experienced disempowerment?

➢ What social representations are informing you, for example as signified in the popular press?

➢ How do you reflexively use your understandings of empowerment in social work?

The complexity of how we must engage in such critical thinking does not end there. In social and political theories there are many debates about each of these social objectives. For example, think about the objective of 'social change' in the IFSW definition of social work. Social change is interpreted and imagined differently across the spectrum of political and ideological perspectives, and there are profound differences in what each perspective will imply about the social world and the various societal institutions of the state, market, individual and collective/community life (Bryson, 1999). Different societies have different historical and cultural patterns and social norms, and these will be in the mix.

For instance, a form of 'conservative imagination', as explored by Thody in his study of conservative authors, has the features of a world view where the emphasis is on what he describes as '... the need for self-discipline and social order' (1993, p. 8). This is clearly not a revolutionary or radical project, and again, with reference to Thody, change is 'careful of jettisoning what we have inherited from the past' (Thody, 1993, p. 165). This is a fundamentally different imagination from the one we imagine as authors of this book. It is different to visions of the type of social change we see is required for empowerment and social justice, which means seeing social structures as profoundly imbued with power inequalities, and where attention needs to be both at the level of structural change and micro level change.

This discussion is of course limited. We give these examples to emphasise that social work is engaged in a process of political imagination and draws on social imaginaries in doing so. Furthermore, social work imaginations of social objectives central to the social work mission do not stand still. Reading widely and reflecting on your ideological perspectives and values and experiences is a resource to the formation of imaginative habits in social work. This can be challenging and sometimes we might not be conscious of deep-seated views until we are pressed. Clare Winnicott writes that '[T]he acquiring of insight during training is a painful process ... involving the shifting of defences, the lessening of rigidity, and the rebuilding of more satisfactory defences based on the insight gained' (2004, Loc 4516 of 5947). Visions are not set in stone as processes of social and political imagining continue and are pushed and pulled by the wider political discursive debates. In Chapter 4 we will come more to habits of imagination that can support these reflexive understandings. Suffice to say, that we have the perpetual challenge to exercise our critical mind and understand what we imagine and mean by these social objectives, and to do this as a coherent practice.

In summary, social work has a long-standing relationship with imagination in many ways. It can facilitate expression, engagement and lighting the beacon of the possible. Imaginative practices in social work are also processes that bring something to life, in the creation of fresh or reformulated understandings and change. These three aspects of imagination for social work – empathy, social imaginaries and imagining social objectives – are depicted in Figure 3.1.

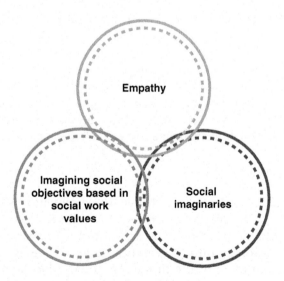

Figure 3.1 Aspects of a social work imagination

C. Wright Mills' sociological imagination

Whilst we have talked in the first part of this chapter about a certain kind of imagination in social work, we now turn to pick up our second use of imagination, which is a way to see what can be taken for granted. You may be familiar with the phrase a 'sociological imagination', coined by the North American sociologist C. Wright Mills writing in the 1950s, and well used in social work literature (Lee, 1994; van Wormer, 2002). Mills defines a sociological imagination as the awareness of the 'interplay of ... intimate settings with their larger structural framework' (1970, p. 179), and attentiveness to how people's private experiences, or 'pains', are connected to the 'public troubles' of the times. This is a capacity or sensibility to locate oneself in '... reference to the historical structures in which the milieux of ... everyday life are organized' (1970, p. 175). He elaborates:

> The sociological imagination, I remind you, in considerable part consists of the capacity to shift from one perspective to another, and in the process to build up an adequate view of a total society and its components. It is this imagination, of course, that sets off the social scientist from the mere technician.
>
> (1970, p. 232)

Each of the social work pioneers in Chapter 2 penned autobiographies, situating themselves in their contexts and times. Alice Salomon neatly captures this spirit of a sociological imagination in her own autobiography, when she situates her 'story' in her historically shaped time:

> The life of a nation is made up of the lives of individuals, and the fate of the individual, passing his early years in the shelter of the family, gradually spreads out into its nation. It is therefore natural that my story begins as a strictly personal narrative and that, as it progresses, national events and the world situation become more distinct while my personal adventures recede and appear like a light pattern on a background of many constantly changing colors.
>
> (2004, p. 247)

Brewer explains Mills gave a map to see 'three dimensions of social reality' (2004, p. 7). The first dimension of the map is a picture that joins the micro world of people's lives and the macro world. The second dimension is a window into time and the role of the past, the here and now, and the unfolding of the future. The final dimension is the workings of power in any society. By thinking about societies in the course of history, social worlds in the course of power relations, and people in the course of their macro worlds, we are, in Mills' terms, engaged in 'sociologically imagining' (Brewer, 2004).

Mills' idea of a sociological imagination has been particularly well taken up in social work, as we said earlier. Indeed, a defining aspect of social work is that we are asked to connect and move between experiences of the macro world, or social structures and the micro world or the everyday lives of individuals, including their internal worlds. This is reflected in the broad canvas of social work practice methods (influencing public policy, community development, group work, case work) and in the International Social Work definition. This is varyingly phrased as joining the 'micro and the macro'; 'the person in the environment'; the 'personal and the political'; in short, social work is an integrated project. This ability to think outside the individual experience/actions is part of the imaginative process Mills outlines. We see this in action in the practice of the social work pioneers we discuss in Chapter 2. Whilst Mills developed his ideas in a particular time and place (Brewer, 2004), and of course ideas move on, they nonetheless give a framework to think about the circumstances of the people we work with in relation to social structural factors, and from this starting point to think about the reasons they engage with social workers, and our own practices.

The social worker is asked to take on a task of conceptual sliding: to reach in our minds to macro understandings and back to the implications for the 'client', and the other way around, from the realities of the client system to what is needed to be different in the macro world: in other words, to reach into the arenas of public policy, politics, economic and social systems. One of the arguments for engaging in sociological social work is to make the connections between what is happening in the society in which we practice, and what we do. This reflects the deeply optimistic nature of social work, with our concern to contribute to better worlds – but we will miss the mark if we do not appreciate the complex dynamics and structures in our globalised world and how they manifest.

Conclusions

A social work imagination such as we are describing can be traced back through time in social work literature, and so well before the time that Mills was writing his work about a sociological imagination (see van Wormer, 2002). We see this in Chapter 2, in the ideals and practices of our social work pioneers. Alice Salomon was a collector of ideas, thoughts and observations and explicitly named the need for habits of

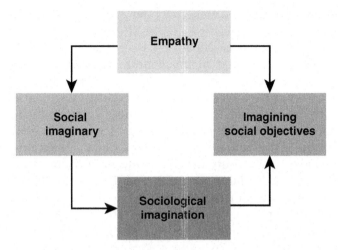

Figure 3.2   Imagination and creativity in practising social work sociologically

attitudes, creativity and imagination. Clare Winnicott talked about imagining links between the micro and the macro and understanding how we develop insight. Jane Addams, activist, social work and Nobel Peace Prize–winner, and Ellen Gates Starr, as described in Chapter 2, were at once creative and sociological in their imaginations. The residents of Hull House were inspired by the nineteenth-century Arts and Crafts movement; this is reflected in the aesthetic of the Hull House environment, with the walls covered with William Morris wallpaper (Morris was a creative socialist, writer and artist), and in the breadth of cultural activities encompassing craft and arts and the use of theatre.

In summary, we can then supplement our framework for social work imagination with a sociological imagination as seen in Figure 3.2. We have three aspects of imagination in practising social work sociologically: empathy, understanding of social imaginaries and the process of imagining social objectives, and lastly, following Mills, a 'sociological imagination'.

In the next chapter we focus on a practice of developing imaginative and creative sensibilities as a habit of imagination in social work.

Practising social work sociologically

As described in this chapter, imagination is a crucial aspect of a practice of sociological social work. Imagination helps us to imagine not only how things might be different but how different people have particular lived experiences that alter from our own. Imagination fuels empathy: it is vital for social work practitioners as well as for the profession. In summary:

➤ imagination is a cognitive process to see a possible and a creative process to make a possible.

➤ empathy is an essential aspect of imagination and fundamental to our social work practice.

➤ Mills called a 'sociological imagination' a process to see connections and patterns in social and cultural processes and people's lives, in order to understand societies and the circumstances of those who live in them.

➤ social work draws on social imaginations about social objectives.

➤ social workers are agents in imaginative processes at two levels: to see and create a possible and see the links between the micro (individual social system) and macro (societal dimensions).

4

Imaginative Sensibilities and Habits

Introduction

A habit of imagination and social work practice is the focus of this next chapter, which extends and builds on what we have discussed in Chapter 3. In this chapter we outline how an imaginative sensibility might become a habit in our social work. Social work pioneer Alice Salomon used the wonderful expression 'habitual attitudes' to designate a quality in her character which called her to action. C. Wright Mills also wrote about the purposeful development of habits. He writes, 'The Sociological Imagination can also be cultivated; certainly it seldom occurs without a great deal of often routine work' (1970, p. 233). Following their lead, and in tune with a broader literature on enabling the release of creativity, in this chapter we come from the position that such habits are a process of rehearsing and fine-tuning to more deeply embed 'imagining' in what we do as social workers.

Social work in an 'iron cage'

In the previous chapter we outlined a case for imaginative sensibilities and habits. Increasingly our social work imaginative wings can find it hard to fly within the requirements of the agencies and organisations where we work (Froggett, 2002; Jackson and Burgess, 2005). Using another metaphor, poet Emily Dickinson's 'possible fuse' can be hard to light and, once lit, a flame that can be easily doused. This can compress space to engage in the sort of social work practice we want to do. The sociologist Max Weber, writing in the early twentieth century, imagined the advance of instrumental rationality and bureaucracy as it was taking shape in the modern world. He conveyed his ideas using a metaphor of an 'iron cage'.

Weber argued a perspective on the influence of the workings of capitalism on individuals within organisations; in brief, that increased rationality and the related structuring of organisations was at the cost of individual expression, and of acting from the heart and spirit. The requirements of a capitalist market system become more important than expression of an individual's creative instincts. Weber writes in *The Protestant Ethic and the Spirit of Capitalism*:

> No one knows who will live in this cage in the future, or whether at the end of this tremendous development entirely new prophets will arise, or there will be a great rebirth of old ideas and ideals or, if neither, mechanized petrification embellished with a sort of convulsive self-importance. ... For of the last stage of this cultural development, it might well be truly said: 'Specialists without spirit, sensualists without heart; this nullity imagines that it has obtained a level of civilization never before achieved'.
>
> (1904/1930, p. 182)

Weber's work is highly applicable to the contemporary landscape in which social work operates today, a point made by sociologists such as Lois Bryson, Anthony Elliott and Charles Lemert (2014). In our earlier work we suggest that contemporary pressures on social work employing organisations can tighten the bars of the cage Weber imagined, or at least result in a feeling that the bars themselves are closing in (Dunk-West and Verity, 2013). These pressures can reduce the 'head space' to even think about how to apply social work's broader values. At the time of writing, in many countries the public policy climate is marked by continuation of 'harsh austerity' policies, as well as resistance to them as evident in the course of the UK General Election in 2017. Like other arenas of public administration, few settings of social work practice have been untouched by market principles and ideas. One very real way this happens is in the requirement to fill in the forms and paperwork required by agencies for accountability purposes. Gillett, Bradfield and Nyland put a numerical value on this accountability in the Australian context. Based on research done in 2011 they estimate accountability requirements could equate to a sector-wide loss 'in excess of 2.7 million hours annually to standards assessment and compliance reporting' (2011, p. 14).

Bolton (2001, p. 3), writing a decade earlier, called these institutional pressures the erosion of the 'right to make moral and professional judgments', happening not just in social work but across other helping professions. This impact of contemporary neo-liberal trends on social work practice has been highlighted time after time in major government-commissioned reports into social welfare in many countries. Eileen Munro, writing on child protection in the United Kingdom, was plain in her stance that: 'The scale of rules and procedures may help achieve a minimum standard of practice, but inhibits the development of professional expertise and alienates the workforce' (Munro Report, 2010, p. 11). The practical realities of the day-to-day implementation of these agendas can be disheartening. Imagining a different way of working can seem out of reach.

Weber's metaphor of an iron cage is the springboard into our discussion of the importance of imagination in social work contexts, but we do not want to minimise or negate the many organisations which actively structure these practices into their organisational design and practices. Furthermore, resident action groups and service user movement groups have much to teach about creativity and imagination. Notwithstanding the above, imagination and imaginative practices are not absent in social work, a point well made by van Wormer (2002), Froggett (2002), Jackson and Burgess (2005) and others. We give some examples here and you will have your own with which you are familiar.

The use of creative expression is the approach taken in a Project called Developing Evidence Enriched Practice (DEEP) in Wales, which has worked creatively with older people, their carers and families, and staff and managers in care homes to explore ways to improve quality. In a Magic Moments project people reflected on 'magic moments' as a means to explore what could be different. In a publication called *Magic Moments in Care Homes*, the authors write:

> Regulation, inspection, guidelines and protocols have a place, but that place is more commonly concerned with organizing and managing services. In the case of 'magic moments', if any attempt is made to over-analyse the moment the magic will be lost ... you can't care plan for them to happen! So we need something very different if we are to create the conditions for magic to happen. We need to adopt a 'glass half full' approach, by asking 'What is it we can do and how can we make it happen?'
>
> (undated, p. 26)

Narrative Therapy, developed at The Dulwich Centre in Adelaide, is another example of the use of creative methods in social work. Here social workers developed a particular approach, therapeutic conversations, using the spoken word but also expression through music and arts (Morgan, ud). One of the advantages of using arts and culture this way is that spaces are created that do not rely solely on words, but engage the senses. This is reminiscent of an idea of the philosopher Wittgenstein that some things are not explainable through words and the grammar of language; they are 'beyond words', sensory and unable to be always articulated in ways that convey the meaning to another. In our own practice we have been involved in social work using drama, puppet making and intergenerational story-telling, murals and concerts. Across all of these projects, without exception, the use of creative means was a way for people to connect with one another outside of a descriptive label of 'client', 'patient, 'service user'; rather the engagement was as human beings connected to one another in a creative process with knowledge to be shared and a collective sense to be formed.

Community Health Onkaparinga (CHO), in an urban Australian local community, provides another example. CHO is a collective comprised of residents and workers who have put creativity at the heart of their work, and use storytelling and creative workshops to capture imaginative ideas for responses to community issues. CHO runs a community gardening project, facilitates meals for women and children in shelters, supports refugees and asylum seekers, and the list goes on. In 2016, CHO set its program of work under the banner of 'Year of the Heart', and began the year with its hopes for the future. As the picture here shows, for one CHO member, their hope drawn into the sand on the beach is that they gain their visa to stay in the country.

Jane Addams, a social work pioneer, linked creativity to the consciousness-raising dimension of theatre at Hull House. As seen in the following extract from a speech given in 1902, Addams situates the lived experiences of the sweatshop workers as a consequence of the industrial revolution, and whilst a structural social worker may argue with the perspective on class exploitation, she illustrates a practice of positioning

Figure 4.1   Sand Drawing: Hope
Source: Photo courtesy of Community Health Onkaparinga (CHO)

experience in a historical context as well as the role of the creative arts in consciousness raising.

> The theater [sic] has been as well a means of education in the broader sense. It has been the means of connecting the lives of the people with the life of the world, not only with that outside of their present environment, but with historical events and achievements. It has served to break up the feeling of isolation. The toilers in the sweat shops for instance, who with their needles are unable to compete with the producers of clothing made by machine labor [sic], have learned that they are not a special class of unfortunates who are being exploited for the benefit of another class of society, but that their experience is only like that of other groups whose industries have been revolutionized by the introduction of machinery.
>
> (http://hullhouse.uic.edu/hull/urbanexp/main.cgi?file=new/ show_doc.ptt&doc=743&chap=100)

As we discuss in Chapter 3, imaginative, analytic and reflexive practice can support social workers to think about and make sense of the times. The role of the imagination in identifying broader social and economic forces helps to contextualise the challenges inherent to social work practice, and is a light to find our way through them.

Exercise

Habits

➢ What is your response to the idea of a 'habit'?

➢ Reflect on how you have formed your own individual habits. Perhaps start with the habits in your daily routine.

➢ Think too about the times when you are trying to change habits and how hard that can be, which reflects unconscious processes and beliefs as much as the other constraints on change.

Imagination in your social work?

➢ How do you engage your imagination in your social work practice?

➢ What supports your imagination?

An order to support imaginative habits

William Morris, mentioned in an earlier chapter, once commented that the productive way to create an effective artistic design was to ensure the presence of three components: beauty, order and imagination. Of 'order' he notes that it is a framework or structure for a design and that it '... *builds a wall against vagueness and opens a door therein for imagination to come in*' (2012, p. 181). Taking on board Morris' idea, we need a structure so we can regularly use imagination, to further develop our imaginative practices, and 'catch and hatch' the ideas and ways of working that come from this thinking. James Angell, a classic writer in the field of psychology, defined imagination as follows:

> Imagination, in the psychologist's meaning, might be called the consciousness of objects not present to the sense. Thus, we can imagine a star we do not see; we can imagine a melody which we do not hear, an odour which we do not actually smell, etc.
>
> (1906, p. 163)

He elaborates that imagination is a quality of mind drawing on what is in our memory bank and what we know from our sensory perceptions, but also that it involves thinking about what we have yet to perceive or experience. He makes the point 'imagining the new' is a process based on what we already know; in other words, imagination can be reproductive and productive. Angell gives an example of imagining an eight-legged dog. From experience, we know what a dogs' leg looks like and, with this image in mind, we can craft a new image of an eight-legged dog (1906, p. 168). Because we don't think it should be left to chance and as we note earlier, mindful of the dulling of imagination that occurs in day-to-day practice, we outline here an order process for support and enrichment of the workings of a social work imagination.

We have been using the term creativity in a general way to refer to the act of sparking and expressing the socially situated imagination. In his work on creativity in primary education, Rupert Wegerif (2010) turns to the work of psychologist Mihaly Csikszentmihalyi and this is a useful lead. Csikszentmihalyi neatly expresses creativity as being in a state of 'flow'. This idea of 'flow' might resonate with you. Csikszentmihalyi describes it as being so caught up in what you are doing that you are unaware of yourself, others, birds singing and time or space. Have you ever had the experience of reading a gripping novel, so absorbing that you can't put it down, even though you might have things to do? Before you realise it time has passed. In Csikszentmihalyi's own words 'flow' is:

> ... the state in which people are so involved in an activity that nothing else seems to matter; the experience itself is so enjoyable that people will do it even at a great cost, for the sheer sake of doing it.
>
> (1990, p. 30)

In this state of being in 'flow', imagination is pumping and creative energies are productive. Csikszentmihalyi's conception of creativity as 'flow' links with the development of the habits or processes of enrichment that we move now to talk about further. As Nakamura and Csikszentmihalyi write, '... experiencing flow encourages a person to persist at and return to an activity because of the experiential rewards it promises, and thereby fosters the growth of skills over time' (2002, p. 96).

We might also use creative methods in our social work, both in how we support people to draw out their experiences and needs, and support them in imagining futures. Jackson and Burgess (2005) describe this comprehensively in their paper on creativity and social work.

An order for creative and imaginative habits in social work

In this section we use the wisdom of C. Wright Mills (1970, pp. 216–248) who provides guidance on how to develop 'habits', a process which he calls 'Intellectual Craftsmanship'. From our reading of Mills we extract four habits he suggests can support imagination which we expand upon: being 'curious', 'drawing comparisons', 'making connexions', and 'surrounding'. We have summarised them as Being **Curious**, Making **Comparisons** and **Connections** and **Surrounding**, in line with the order William Morris writes about, an order to establish and to maintain habits of imagination in social work. We can add them to our imagination schema as shown in Figure 4.2.

Curiosity

In the broad literature on imagination it is common to read about curiosity. Mills intrinsically places a curious disposition at the heart of his sociological imagination. However, as he writes, this needs to be accompanied by a means 'to capture what you experience and sort it out' (1970, p. 216). Capturing or holding insights, questions and experiences so you can make sense of them is a familiar strategy in social work where we are encouraged to engage in reflective analysis and use tools like reflective diaries, regular reflection groups, social work supervision (Gould and Taylor, 1996; Dunk-West, 2013). It is not just social workers who do this; this is a common practice in a range of disciplines. Mills says this disposition or habit of curiosity:

'... also encourages you to capture "fringe-thoughts": various ideas which may be by-products of everyday life, snatches of conversation overheard on the

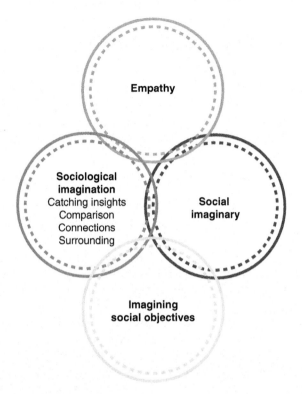

Figure 4.2   Shaking up thinking

street, or, for that matter, dreams'. Once noted, these may lead to more system-atic thinking, as well as lend intellectual relevance to more directed experience.

(1970, pp. 216–217)

There is much written about this focus on curiosity and imagination. Michael Gelb in his book *How to Think like Leonardo da Vinci* outlines da Vincian principles, the first of which is 'curiosita' or the 'desire to learn more'. Gelb explains this principle to be the character of having an open and inquiring attitude towards people, nature, society, experiences and knowledge, and a commitment to wonder and learn. He cites an entry from Leonardo da Vinci's diary where da Vinci writes: 'when you are out for a walk, see to it that you watch and consider other men's [*sic*] postures and actions as they talk, argue, laugh or scuffle; their own actions, and those of their supporters and onlookers: and make a note of these with a few strokes in your little notebook which you must always carry with you' (Gelb, 2004, pp. 74–75).

Social worker and researcher Alice Salomon, introduced in Chapter 2, is described by many writers as someone who lived a curious existence. She gives an example in her autobiography *Character is Destiny*, where hearing a factory whistle takes her thoughts back to her reading of Tolstoy and to his ideas about inequality and justice:

> Tolstoy's *What Then Shall We Do?* became my textbook. It taught me to see the wrongs we inflict on others through sheer carelessness, and even now I cannot hear a factory whistle calling the employees to work before dawn without thinking of his powerful contrast between the lives of the rich and the poor. It has done more for me than many a course in social psychology can do for a social worker.
>
> (2004, pp. 32–33)

The essence of a curious disposition is the open-mindedness which van Wormer (2002), Jackson and Burgess (2005) and our social work pioneers describe so well. This means we do not approach our social work practice with preconceptions, or a priori assumptions about what is, or what and how things should be. This is not to say we do not have clear values, but rather that they are combined with a sense of wonder and inquiry.

There are many practices for supporting curiosity, and some of these are dialogical strategies based on the premise that we can extend this sensibility when we engage with and talk with others (Wegerif, 2010). These processes can spark thoughts that are we are 'yet to think'. They can be informal practices and just naturally what you do with others, or it might be more formalised. You might recall the Social Science Club, an organised process of lectures and dialogue run by Hull House residents that Jane Addams writes enthusiastically about. There are many formal dialogical approaches, and these include Appreciative Inquiry and other methods of collectively talking and deeply exploring. For instance the Appreciative Inquiry model, pared back to its essence, is a strengths-based approach to exploration and dialogue which revolves around 4 steps, or phases: 'discovery'; 'dreaming together'; and 'designing' what might be to create a 'destiny' (Cooperrider and Whitney, 2005). The strengths-based approach which underpins Appreciative Inquiry aligns with social work perspectives. As Watkins et al. write, it is a '... process of seeking to understand through asking questions' (2011, p. 22). Supervision and group reflective practices are also opportunities to explore what we think through deep discussions.

Cynthia Cockburn, in the following extract, explains the place of imagination in dialogical processes, and note her reference to taking a 'leap into the dark' and to 'dreams of possibilities':

> The belief that you and I will be different ten years from now, and that our circumstances will allow different practices, demands imagination. So we cannot

do trans-versal politics, we cannot even make the first steps, without a leap into the dark. Our politics must not just allow space for, but actively generate, flights of fantasy, dreams of possibilities. The traversing is thus not only lateral, it is also traversing into the future (yours and hers).

(2015, p. 5)

Whilst each dialogical approach might well have a distinctive technique, in common will be the aim to facilitate discussion spaces for people to come together to communicate with one another. This takes openness, time and curiosity, and the commitment to empathy which we talked about earlier in Chapter 3.

Exercise

It may be that being curious is part of your own character and you have maintained your childhood sense of asking why (Why can't we feel gravity or that the Earth is spinning?), and being interested in what you see and what is happening around you. However, for many of us this can change as we engage in processes of socialization.

What nourishes your curious spirit?

Think about how your feel and think about curiosity?

Drawing comparisons and making connections

Social work practice has increasingly been organised to divide human existence and experience into separate 'issues', 'age groups', 'locations', 'fields, e.g., health or social care, and other categories. Partly this has emerged with specialisation and it is also a response to how services are funded and organised. Each area develops and deepens its own concepts, acronyms, approaches, evidence base, and whilst there is of course a valid place for specialisation and sensitive and knowledgeable responses to certain needs, a downside is that it can impede making connections across these divisions to the common socially shaped patterns. Sometimes the language used can be completely alienating and it is not a surprise then this can impede shared understandings; it might simply be we do not know what is being said. Because of this, we need to work harder to see patterns and connections; the implications for the realisation of social work goals of justice and empowerment can be shadowy thoughts rather than directly in the light.

Mills advised the importance of 'making connexions' between various experiences and thoughts, between what we read, see, hear and feel. The example above from Alice Salomon illustrates this practice of drawing connections, in her case from what she was reading to the sound of a factory whistle blowing. This also has a temporal element. We can seek connections backwards and forward across periods of time, and it can also mean connections across space to what happens in different contexts, and between different imaginations in our mind-eyes which we will have stored away. Mills writes, 'Imagination is often successfully invited by putting together hitherto isolated items, by finding unsuspected connexions' (1970, p. 221).

Related is what he proposes as a practice of loosening up rigid thinking and opening up imagination by rearranging our own mental and real-world filing cabinets. Mills says, 'You simply dump out heretofore disconnected folders, mixing up their contents, and then re-sort them' (1970, p. 233). He is referring to shaking up the very structure of the system of how we have organised notes and ideas; then we can see a different pattern or picture. This can lead to new insights that transcend what is already noted and then filed away.

Exercise

➢ How can you shake up your thinking?

➢ At a systems level governments can organise themselves in ways which can create silos and inhibit the ease of seeing and making connections. Think about the sector and agency you work in. How well do people work across disciplines or sectors?

In social work, making connections can also be developed by connecting aspects of social work with other disciplines and creative endeavours. This may be through poetry, or literature, but it could also be many other areas of work or life – gardening and social work, or nature and social work. William Morris, who we mention earlier, is an example of a person who made connections with the aesthetic and the practical, economic and community, literature and politics.

Once we start to make connections we then can see how things are in other places to the ones we know (geographic, temporal, and place as 'perspective' or experience). This is one of the key ideas in Edward de Bono's work on lateral thinking, or seeking of alternatives. Mills

Figure 4.3   Shaking up thinking

emphasised considering extremes and trying to catch the '... light from as many angles as possible' (1970, pp. 235–236). He writes:

> If you think about despair, then also think about elation; if you study the miser, then also the spendthrift.
>
> (1970, p. 235)

and:

> The release of imagination can sometimes be achieved by deliberately inverting your sense of proportion. If something seems very minute, imagine it to be simply enormous, and ask yourself: What difference might that make? And vice-versa, for gigantic phenomena.
>
> (1970, p. 236)

This is particularly helpful to see the patterns of how certain ideas and interests are having an impact on social work, and the shared nature of these impacts. For example, the impact of neo-liberal policies, where there has been a withdrawal of state activity in directly providing services

---

Exercise

A starting point is to read and hear about how social work is being practised across the world and in other settings, as Alice Salomon and Jane Addams did.

➢ What is happening in the setting of your practice? How is social work organised?

➢ How does it compare with social work practised in other settings?

➢ How does it contrast to social work practised in times past?

---

an outsourced model of delivery is common to many OECD countries. Through this comparison, it may be observed that what is occurring in your setting is part of something wider and more pervasive than just your agency's practice, or the ideas of the organisational leaders. It sits in a social, political and historical context.

Surrounding

The practice of what Mills calls '... surrounding oneself by a circle of people who will listen and talk – and at times they have to be imaginary characters' (Mills, 1970, p. 222) again, is a commonplace strategy in the literature on the development of creativity and imagination. It is the purposeful practice of being in imaginative and creative environments, such as being around supportive people who can spark our thinking and encourage our reflective habits. Such 'surrounding' can be an encouragement and help us loosen ourselves, as it were, so we can test out ideas, pose puzzles and questions (Bolton, 2001; Jackson and Burgess, 2005). Jackson and Burgess (2005, p. 10) call this 'sources of stimulation' for creativity. Jenny Uglow (2002) depicts a form of this surrounding practice in her book entitled *The Lunar Men: The Friends Who Made the Future:* friends, who were writers and inventors of the European Enlightenment period who met at a set time on a Monday after the full moon to talk, share a meal, imagine and invent. They include Josiah Wedgewood, a member of the pottery family, James Watts, who invented the steam engine, and the inventor Erasmus Darwin, the grandfather of Charles Darwin. What is pertinent in Uglow's account is how these friends maintained their curiosity; they surrounded themselves with one another. She writes:

> Amid fields and hills the Lunar men build factories, plan canals, make steam-engines thunder. They discover new gases, new minerals and new medicines

and propose unsettling new ideas. They create objects of beauty and poetry of bizarre allure. They sail on the crest of the new. Yet their powerhouse of invention is not made up of aristocrats or statesmen or scholars but of provincial manufacturers, professional men and gifted amateurs – friends who meet almost by accident and whose lives overlap until they die.

(xiii–xiv)

Uglow's story of the *Lunar Men* is about friends from different fields supporting each other in creativity and inventiveness. This was as much a collective project as it was about individual pursuits. Yet the 'Enlightenment' period was not just about the inventive spirit that Uglow describes, but a profoundly disturbing historical period of oppression and suffering for many people, whose liberty and lands were taken to produce the new products of the industrial era. For many of the people who worked in mills and factories their living and working conditions were harsh. Activists and social reformers like William Wilberforce and Octavia Hill were also surrounding themselves with others, joining together with an emerging social imaginary, determination and solidarity about addressing oppression and working for social and human rights that were denied in the new economic development. In these campaigns for rights and justice, activists surrounded themselves with each other, as part of their imaginative, determined work for human rights, justice and political expression.

As social workers we are engaged in creative and inventive work that matters (van Wormer, 2002; Froggett, 2002; Jackson and Burgess, 2005). Surrounding ourselves with sources of motivation and encouragement, and 'cultivating humanity' will help us keep our social work imaginative fuse glowing. We might do this through supervision, being part of groups to talk and think about social work practice, dilemmas, our passion for social justice and what could be different. We get stimulation outside of our work as well. Clare Winnicott had a particular emphasis on creative work, not surprising given her work with children and families, and she expresses in her writing the importance of a social worker surrounding themselves with enrichment. She writes:

> Friendships, reading, and cultural activities of all kinds, and holidays, all enrich our lives and knowledge of the world and of ourselves. We know that every situation in which we can be ourselves, and enjoy ourselves, not only adds another dimension to life, but liberates us for further experiences. Our personal life is the base from which we operate and to which we return. The firmer the base, the freer we are to make excursions into the unknown.
>
> (Chapter 12 herein. Loc 2044 of 5947)

Surrounding practices are not confined to an explicit social work-focused agenda. Think about how you gain inspiration and its relation to your own insights and internal questioning. Jane Addams writes of the *'inspiration and solace of literature'*. You might find this is a source for you, or it could be through cinema, attending talks and places where people talk about ideas, or watching Ted Talks and staying engaged in public debates and community and social movements. It may also be through faith and engagement with the natural world. You will know what it is for you. Fundamentally we do this with a curiosity about the social worlds in which we live, and curiosity about our own purpose and practice.

Conclusions

Sociological social work practice is supported by a habit of imagination, but it also depends on engagement with ideas or theoretical constructs which can help order our thinking and analysis, and in the remainder of the book our focus is how ideas can be applied in practice.

Practising social work sociologically

The use of imagination can be routinely reflected upon and practised, both actively in day-to-day life and within social work practice. In this chapter we have explored some of the ways in which imagination is realised and we have discussed the contemporary world in which social work takes place as an important anchor for thinking about alternatives and possibilities. In summary, this chapter has explored the following:

➤ Imagination is displayed across all areas of human experience and is part of social work, which is fundamentally an imaginative field of practice.

➤ Habits or imaginative sensibilities can support us to root a spirit of imagination in our practice.

➤ Imaginative habits can be developed through an order or structure.

➤ C. Wright Mills' (1970) craft of a 'Sociological Imagination' gives us a structure for imaginative habits in social work practice.

    o Be curious.

    o Draw comparisons and make connections.

    o Surround yourself with sources of support and enrichment.

5

Self, Agency and Structure

Introduction

In this chapter we examine the social work concept of agency or self-determination, alongside identity. We also examine the concept of social structure and the role of society in shaping individual experiences and choices. Firstly, we explore the meaning of the term 'identity' as it relates to the ways in which social workers think about the world around them, alongside the meaning of this for their work with clients. The notion of reflexivity is examined as it relates to social work identity. We argue that existing theories of reflexivity, as they relate to social work learning, draw from a particular framework. Symbolic Interactionist theories of identity are therefore explored as they relate to identity development in social work. We then move on to consider the concept of agency or self-determination. The tension between the individual and the social is a focus of this chapter and the complexity between these two terms is explored. The chapter concludes by outlining the ways in which the tension between agency and structure are borne out in social work practice.

Identity/self

As we have seen so far in this book, a dominant image in the contemporary landscape in which individuals are immersed is a focus on the self. Sociological theories help us connect together individual characteristics and experiences in order to better understand social phenomena. Yet what do we mean when we isolate the individual from society? Can we or should we do this in social work? The answers to these questions are complex. This is because we live in a time when the individual has come to the forefront when we examine issues pertinent to human experience. Firstly, it is important to understand what we mean when we discuss the 'individual'.

Identity categories

Names for 'identity' depend upon the discipline or profession in which the concept is being explored. The following list relates to similar meanings, for example:

➤ Subjectivity

➤ Self

➤ Identity

➤ Individual

All of these terms depict a focus on one person as opposed to a collection of individuals which might make up, for example, a family, social group, community or society. Before moving on to consider the degree to which others have a 'choice' in acting against social expectations, it is important to recognise the role of reflexivity in conceptualisations of the individual and, in turn, social work.

Reflexivity is different from reflecting. Reflexivity means that insights gained from reflection are consciously applied to future action. Say an individual decides that they would like to be known as a better driver. They may reflect on their driving record, their existing skills and decide that they don't feel comfortable driving in particular conditions. Once identifying a gap in knowledge, the individual might decide that they need more education. The person might then decide to undertake a driving course to get skills in off-road driving which supplements their existing skills and helps them achieve their desire to become a better driver. This is an example of reflexivity. Insights from reflection – thinking about gaps in knowledge or skills, or a desire for a new 'identity' are actioned through reflexive anticipation of the future.

In social work education, reflexivity has long been seen as the means through which social work students understand themselves in a professional context. The placement is the process whereby reflexivity is practised, particularly through the supervisory process. Students reflect on their practice and think about what they could have said/ not said or acted differently to bring about a better outcome. Similarly, pre-placement topics require students to think about their communication skills and reflect upon their ethical and value-base. Let's take a look at how social work has conceptualised reflexivity and begin to unravel some of the underpinning assumptions behind the location of reflexivity in professional identity formation. We show that symbolic interactionism helps to counter some of the assumptions about identity formation in social work and offers a complementary theoretical framework for learning and identity generation in social work.

Reflexivity in social work

It is often difficult to conceptualise the ways in which the social work placement fits with other types of knowledge acquisition during students' education about social work. The placement is 'different' to classroom-based learning. It is an important opportunity for students to apply classroom-based knowledge to the 'real world'. Here theory and practice 'come together' and this process has been explained through the use of the concepts of 'integration' and reflexivity; often interchangeably. Integration refers to the ways in which practice and theory unite in a student's practice. As noted earlier, reflexivity, in this sense, refers to the process whereby students reflect upon past practice, think about what theories 'fit' and anticipate future action in relation to their practice and theory useage (Bogo and Vayda, 1987; Healy, 2005). Integration and reflexivity require students to undertake imaginative deliberations in which practice is recalled and recoded according to the particular skills, models and theories which inform their interactions with clients. This kind of process draws from the work of theorists for whom reflection and reflexivity produce a new kind of knowledge which can be taken into social workers' future interactions (see, e.g., Bogo and Vayda, 1987).

The problem with reflexivity in social work is its varied meanings and applications where reflexivity can be concerned with 'a response to an immediate context ... [or] an individual's self-critical approach ... [or] ... concerned with the part that emotion plays in social work practice' (D'Cruz et al., 2007, p. 75). These permutation of reflexivity require social workers or social work students to actively engage in this process; it is neither a by-product of practice nor an automatically ascribed process. As we shall see later in the chapter, a new configuration of reflexivity which draws from sociological insights into identity can help to shift this discourse.

In relation to reflexivity but also to the social work placement itself, there is a dearth of literature in which the psychoanalytic model of self is critiqued in social work. Psychoanalytic theories of self draw from unconscious or unrecognised processes which are part of the subjective, the internal processes concerned with which are separate from social functioning. Although there is much to be gained in exploring this kind of self, ultimately we need to understand the role that reflexivity has alongside an appreciation of agency, as we explore later in this chapter. For example, Miehls and Moffatt argue that social workers ought to '...

work on a reflexive self' (p. 339) and highlight the subjective meanings produced through social interaction (Miehls and Moffatt, 2000). This goes some way to promote sociality as central to social work self-production. Sociality refers to the social interactions, communications and processes which both constitute and reflect people's identities.

Symbolic interactionism and the self

George Herbert Mead's (Mead, 1913) conceptualisation of self provides a theoretical model in which social work can shift the focus from individuals to broader society and the external 'other' of the profession itself (Dunk-West, 2013b). Firstly, it is important to understand how the focus on the individual social work student helps to make sense of how social work educational components come together.

What Mead brings to social work resonates with an existing orthodoxy in which society is central in shaping individual circumstance. Rejecting popular psychological models of identity, Mead instead argues that the self is generated through social interaction (Mead, 1913) rather than contained 'within'. The process of understanding the attitudes of broader society is ongoing from birth and eventually anticipated through imagined interaction. He says:

> The self arises in conduct, when the individual becomes a social object in experience to himself. This takes place when the individual assumes the attitudes or uses the gesture which another individual would use and responds to it himself, or tends so to respond. It is a development that arises gradually in the life of the infant ... he talks to himself in a manner analogous to that in which he acts towards others. Especially he talks to himself as he talks to others and in keeping up this conversation in the inner forum constitutes the field which is called that of mind.
>
> (Mead, 1922, p. 67)

Shifting the focus away from the 'internal' mind, Mead instead highlights the significance of the social in self constitution. For example, Mead argues that in childhood firstly play and then games help actors to learn how to anticipate society's response to their actions. During play, children take on the socially recognised roles they see around them: for example, playing 'Mum' or 'Doctor' (Mead, 1925, pp. 80–81). After children achieve mastery over playing roles, they move on to interact with one another through participating in games. Games have a structure and rules and require the player to anticipate other players' responses. These processes prepare the child for interaction in the adult world. Mead says:

In the process of communication the individual is an other before he is a self. It is in addressing himself in the role of an other that his self arises in experience. The growth of the oragnized [*sic*] game out of simple play in the experience of the child, and of organized group activities in human society, placed the individual then in a variety of roles, in so far as these were parts of the social act, and the very organization of these in the whole act gave them a common character in indicating what he had to do. He is able then to become a generalized other in addressing himself in the attitude of the group or the community. In this situation he has become a definite self over against the social whole to which he belongs.

(Mead, 1926, p. 199)

Despite the emphasis on the self, Mead's is not a model which resonates with individualisation or the 'project of self' (Giddens, 1990, 1991) in which actors' reflexivity involves an inward focus and an orientation towards self-improvement. By utilising Mead's theory of self, broader social norms, practices, structures and institutions are illuminated. In contemporary social work, the means to highlight inequality, oppression and social norms is important. This requires students to conform to social work's ethical and political stance. Again, this highlights the socialisation process and shifting self which occurs during social work education. Mead says

As a mere organization of habit the self is not self-conscious. It is this self which we refer to as character. When, however, an essential problem appears, there is some disintegration in this organization, and different tendencies appear in reflective thought as different voices in conflict with each other. In a sense the old self has disintegrated, and out of the moral process a new self arises.

(Mead, 1913, p. 61)

Mead's work in which social control is theorised is helpful when considering social work education and our examination of the individual and reflexivity. The 'generalised other' is the norms and values from a given society. During the early years, each child internalises these until they can predict society's reaction to their own behaviour: in this way the generalised other mediates and is a form of social control. However, 'social control, then, will depend upon the degree to which the individual does assume the attitudes of those in the group who are involved with him in his social activities' (Mead, 1925, p. 84). There is a social work corollary to be drawn from this.

Through the process of professional identity formation in social work, teaching staff aim to impart social work norms and values to their students. These norms are dependent on national, local and institutional practices and differences, as well as broader concepts such as social justice.

As noted earlier (and in previous work; see, e.g., Dunk-West, 2013b) reflexivity has received much attention in social work. In Mead's conception of self, reflexivity is embedded in the emergence of self through social interaction. Such a theory of reflexivity bears out a different emphasis in social work education and learning.

Mead's theory of self brings a sociological approach to the idea of reflexivity, particularly in terms of the ways in which it highlights sociality as required for the creation of self (see, e.g., Dunk-West, 2012, 2013a, 2013b). Accepting Mead's theory of self requires social work to look at reflexivity through a critical lens. As noted earlier, existing permutations of reflexivity in social work draw from psychoanalytic models of self, albeit to varying degrees. The idea that if the student just focuses hard enough, they will discover hidden aspects of self underappreciates the social influences on self which are present from the onset of social work education.

Imagine, instead, a curriculum in which reflexivity forms part of a pedagogy in which self-constitution is a by-product of social interaction. This is a reorientation in pedagogy, and has implications for the ways in which the social work placement is differentiated from university-based learning. From the beginning of the social work curriculum, students are encouraged to communicate with one another, whether as a group or team for an assessment exercise or as a 'cohort' of students who relate to one another through problem-solving activities relating to case studies, applying theory to 'real-life' scenarios and engaging in dialogue with one another. If we think about Mead's theory of childhood and the ways in which society's norms and values are 'internalised' firstly through play and then through games, a translation into social work education is evident. The interactions between students and their teachers, practice educators, even the theories and ideas represented in the social work canon are all examples of social interactions which tell students what social work means. Common themes in the values which underpin social work are threaded through each of these examples.

Let us now move on to consider a neglected aspect of social work selfhood which is related to reflexivity: the consideration and manifestation of time in the social work curriculum and pedagogical models. We discuss time in Chapter 7; however, time ought to be considered in relation to the 'making' of a social worker and the role of reflexivity. Whereas reflexivity models require a clearly differentiated notion of past, present and future, in Mead's conceptualisation of the self, time is *mediated through the present* (Mead, 1929). Mead says:

The past is an overflow of the present. It is oriented from the present. It is akin on the one side to our escape fancies, those in which we rebuild the world according to our hearts' desires, and on the other to the selection of what is significant in the immediate situation, the significant that must be held and reconstructed, but its decisive character is the pushing back of the conditioning continuities of the present. The past is what must have been before it is present in experience as a past. A past triumph is indefinitely superior to an escape fancy, and will be worn threadbare before we take refuge in the realm of the imagination, but more particularly the past is the sure extension which the continuities of the present demand.

(Mead, 1929, p. 206)

Such a conceptualisation of time has a bearing on the 'making' of a social worker in three significant ways. Firstly, whereas integration and reflexivity models rely upon clear delineation between the past, present and future, using Mead's theory of self, time becomes significant in the present and the emphasis is upon the relations in which the self, across time, emerges. Secondly, reflexivity is automatically embedded into self-making rather than a deliberate process in Mead's theory of self. Thirdly, it is important to recognise that as soon as social work students commence their studies, they are in the process of becoming a social worker. Placement is therefore equally as important to professional self-making as is classroom-based learning and, crucially, the interaction which occurs within the classroom. Interactions between teaching staff, fellow students, help to solidify Mead's 'generalised other', or the values and beliefs, of the profession. There is therefore a further analysis of time, which ought to be fleshed out, and which has forbearance upon our argument.

Historically, community and understanding contemporary society and its practices and injustices have been at the forefront of social work. The conceptualisation of collectivism helped early figures in social work both understand the social and inform the method in which they worked to create positive change. In more recent times there has been a marked re-orientation towards more individualist models of society and identity. This has had an impact upon the ways in which social work views itself as a profession as well as the ways in which pedagogy is understood. The social work placement has been the site at which social work students have been encouraged to reflect upon and alter their selves through a kind of reflexivity which has its roots in what Furedi terms 'therapy culture' (Furedi, 2004), that is, through drawing in a psychoanalytic model of subjectivity. It is therefore important to understand reflexivity in its predominantly uncritical position in social work education through this lens of history. Individualist narratives have arisen in social work to coincide with the emphasis and proliferation of the concepts which have grown from theories stemming from the concept of psychoanalytic subjectivity. More recently, reflexivity is argued to have grown out of the conditions of the present, in which globalised and technologically innovative and shifting landscapes reign (Giddens, 1991). Yet inequalities continue to exist in this terrain (Heaphy, 2007).

Reflection and reflexivity are overwhelmingly noted in social work literature as useful, important and as processes which ought to be practised throughout one's career. Yet there is little critical appreciation of the model of self from which these concepts stem. In practice, students are encouraged to operationalise reflection and reflexivity in a compartmentalised manner in which the past is reflected upon as separate from the present, and the future. When we adopt a social model of self, such as through adopting George Herbert Mead's theory of self, reflexivity is broadened and reliant upon social interaction rather than thought processes. Instead of an acceptance of the past informing present behaviour, such as in therapeutic discourses, in social work we need to reconceptualise time in relation to a social model of self. Recall of practice events, then, ought to be embedded in the present, despite their status as 'past'. As Mead says:

> Imagery is not past but present. It rests with what we call our mental processes to place these images in a temporal order. We are engaged in spreading backward what is going on so that the steps we are taking will be a continuity in the advance to the goals of our conduct.
>
> (Mead, 1929, p. 205)

In adopting Mead's configuration of self-constitution in social work, we downgrade the importance of reflexivity as a deliberate process and we elevate the importance of sociality in the social work educative environment. Thus, the placement becomes equally as important as other opportunities for social interaction. Additionally, the idea that reflexivity is relevant primarily to one's practice with clients limits our appreciation of self-making in social work.

Now that we have considered professional identity and the role of classroom-based and placement learning alongside reflexivity, we will move on to consider the notion of agency – or one's ability to act freely. The degree to which a person (actor) has freedom is something that is contested in sociology. In social work, there has been a clear value placed on the notion of self-determination: many ethical codes from varying national contexts note that this ethical concept ought to shape social work practice in that social workers are encouraged to promote client self-determination. Yet to what degree are clients able to act freely? To follow our previous example of an individual wanting to become a 'better driver', what if an individual would like to become the next Prime Minister? Is this equally possible for everyone or do social inequalities related to identity categories such as culture, age, educational background and sexual identity play a part in reducing the amount of 'choice' someone has in shaping their future?

Agency

Agency relates to an individual's ability to exercise choice in the context of their circumstances. Agency can also be traced in relation to patterns of 'choice' people have. For example, Jeanette Winterson offers the following quote about the ability of women to make choices in societies where they experience inequality:

> *Hox is a racing word: it means to hamstring a horse not so brutally that she can't walk but cleverly so that she can't run. Society hoxes women and pretends that God, Nature or the genepool designed them lame.*
>
> Winterson (1995, p. 62)

The tension between agency and structure is one of the enduring debates in sociology. The degree to which an individual has control or choice over their actions, behaviours and participation in society's institutions is affected to a large extent by the power relationships and environments in which they are immersed. Yet the notion of empowerment and self-determination are also at the heart of social work practice. How do we reconcile the differences between these two? Social work students and those new to practice often describe their helping role as 'empowering others'. Yet how do social workers 'empower'? And why has empowerment become the response to the tension between individual choice and social expectations? Can one be 'empowered' if they are in a disempowering situation? Why don't social workers seek to disempower those who misuse power?[1] It is not enough to expect that social workers can empower individuals without other forms of intervention at structural levels. As McDonald notes:

> Failing to acknowledge the dramatic restructure of welfare can result in a form of magical thinking wherein people have difficulty accepting the realities of the contemporary world, and as a result cannot engage in ways that find real purchase. And it is this purchase that critical social workers need to

---

[1] Source: Social work academics Dr Kate Seymour and Dr Heather Fraser are acknowledged in this line of argument, as they have provided many critical conversations about empowerment and power.

find if critical social work is going to survive. Effective critical social work in the current workfare world has three essential components: a critical analysis; critical reflexivity combined with a critical consciousness; and critical politics.

(McDonald, 2009, p. 245)

Yet how can a social worker use a critical lens to enable them to see both the individual and the social concurrently? Firstly, the social worker requires an understanding of structural issues.

Social structure

The concept of structure helps social scientists to better understand influences in individuals which influence 'choice'. Social structure can appear to be somewhat of a difficult concept to 'pin down' (Sewell, 1992) as it is a concept rather than an object. Giddens and Sutton refer to social structure as: 'patterns of interaction between individuals, groups and institutions' noting that 'most of our activities are structured: they are organized in a regular and repetitive way' (Giddens and Sutton, 2013, p. 1071). This definition helps to frame the interactive nature of the individual and the social: the individual acts in particular ways which then produces structure which has the potential to 'constrain *and* make possible individuals' actions' (Inglis, 2012).

It is a matter of consistent debate the degree to which individuals are able to change structure. Thus, 'agency versus structure' is an enduring point of scholarly debate in sociology. This debate seeks to explore or explain in which ways individual decisions are shaped by broader patterns of interaction of which the individual is often unaware. Social structure is pervasive in social life:

> Whatever aspect of social life we designate as structure is posited as 'structuring' some other aspect of social existence – whether it is class that structures politics, gender that structures employment opportunities, rhetorical conventions that structure texts or utterances, or modes of production that structure social formations.
>
> (Sewell, 1992)

In sociology there are many traditions, some are contradictory and others fall within the same ontological framework. This can make it difficult to argue that 'sociology says X about Y'. There is a range of theoretical perspectives in sociology and each has its own conceptualisation of individuals and society. Critical theorists argue that social change needs to occur through collective action or revolution whereas a symbolic interactionist approach might argue that individual expressions, gestures and actions feed in to social structure – so if these change, then the social can also change accordingly. Although this is somewhat of an oversimplification, it is important to note that there are many conflicting perspectives in sociology. Yet what *can* be said is that sociology is a discipline which is interested in better understanding social structure. The interest in social structure is realised through the diverse traditions which have theorised particular social structures. For example, see the following table, in which we have given some examples of the different approaches and the social structure theorised.

SOCIAL STRUCTURE	EXAMPLE OF AN ASSOCIATED TRADITION	ASSOCIATED THEORIST
Religion	Macro/interpretivist	Weber
Economic system	Critical/conflict theories	Marx
Knowledge/power	Aligned with post-structural approaches	Foucault
Gender and race	Feminist/intersectionality	bell hooks
Class	Cultural theory	Bourdieu

Table 5.1   Social Structure, Theoretical Traditions and Theorists

What is important about structure? And how are theories of structure relevant to social work? When we think about the people with whom we work, we often assume that 'change' is possible. Understanding the limiting conditions that structures perpetuate is an important insight which we can use in our work. It is sometimes assumed that people are able to 'choose' freely: understanding structure helps to conceptualise the potential blockages that people encounter on a day-to-day basis. Understanding that choice is determined by a range of social factors helps us to better advocate and empathise with our clients. It also helps when we are addressing structural inequalities (Mullaly, 1997).

Conclusions

In this chapter we have explored the idea of identity and structure and the constraints to the choice narrative that dominates in the contemporary world. We have examined the 'making' of a social worker by understanding the micro processes which constitute professional self-making. Reflexivity in social work is firmly grounded in our professional roles and supervision and we have explored how this concept relates to social work selfhood. Reflexivity has been examined in this chapter as a counter to the idea that if we just try hard enough or set goals for ourselves, then change will occur. Our exploration of structure and structural inequalities suggests that this idea of complete agency is counter to this narrative.

Practising social work sociologically

Practising social work sociologically in relation to self, agency and structure involves better understanding the expectations that are placed on the individual when we promote change. Reflexivity has been explored in the context of social work education and learning as well as examined in relation to symbolic interactionist traditions which see the individual as an ongoing relationship with their surrounds. In summary, the following are examples of the ways in which social work can be practised sociologically in relation to identity and agency and social structure:

> ➤ understanding theories of identity which draw upon scholarship in relation to social and historical contexts

> ➤ understanding that reflexivity is part of a broader cultural shift towards individual experience

> ➤ understanding that empowerment is problematic if it does not take into account social structure

> ➤ understanding that social work must be oriented toward social structure and use approaches which respond to both individual and social issues.

6

Social Relationships and 'Capital'

Introduction

In this chapter we examine the relationship between individuals, the multiple 'communities' and social groupings in which they are located and at the same time consider the role that broader society has in shaping individual experience. Locating the individual within their social contexts and systems is important in social work, as was evident in our discussion of social work pioneers Alice Salomon, Clare Winnicott and Jane Addams. In exploring the relation between human experience and the constitution of society, early sociologist Georg Simmel makes the point that 'Individuals and society are, both for historical understanding and for normative judgement, *methodological concepts*' (1971, p. 37). Yet what does this mean for social work? We believe that it is important for social workers to be able to locate the individual alongside others. This tradition is inherent to social work historically, and reflects a broader interest not only in the individual, but an interest in society which is always present in social work.

By understanding broader social patterns and consistencies in thinking about individuals and about societies, we are able to better understand the individual as one person intricately linked within their social contexts. It is therefore important to examine social connectedness and social relationships and we explore this in this chapter. In understanding the ways in which individuals seek meaning, identity and support through social relationships, we apply sociological theory to social work knowledge and practice. Social development, supports and connectedness, social isolation or social exclusion are important to frame within theoretical knowledge that explains the modern-day world and the challenges it brings to the individual in maintaining social bonds. Drawing from Bourdieu's work on social and cultural capital, the concepts of social relatedness and 'community' are therefore examined in this chapter and related to particular ways that we make sense of society and the individual's role in participating in social interactions, and the social work role in supporting stronger communities and social networks. The first task of this chapter is to critically explore the rise of the narrative of the individual and to highlight that this is a relatively new phenomenon.

Exercise

In recent times, we have seen a shift in professionals' focus to the individual. The rise of neuroscience is an example of the ways in which the individual is seen as 'containing' the answers to individual issues.

➤ What, if any, influence does the social have on the individual?

➤ What is a consequence of the increased interest in the individual?

Public narrative of the individual

In contemporary society there has been a marked increase in the ways in which we make sense of the diversity of human experience. The use of therapy, for example, has increased markedly in modern times and is often the first place people are advised to turn to when one is faced with adversity. As Furedi points out:

> Today, with the rise of the confessional mode, the blurring of the line between the private and the public and the powerful affirmation for emotionalism, there is little doubt that it has become a formidable cultural force. Its power is demonstrated through its influence on popular culture.
>
> (Furedi, 2004, p. 17)

Here, Furedi refers to the proliferation of self-help texts, reality shows and popular magazines as the pervasive discourses which frame emotional experiences such as anxiety, grief, trauma and risk. *Your Erroneous Zones*, a self-help book by Wayne Dyer, with a byline 'escape negative thinking and turn your life around', has sold thirty-five million copies. It is somewhat radical to think about the idea that therapy is part of a broader cultural shift which highlights the individual's cognition, emotion and places it at the centre. Yet Furedi's scholarship helps to critically analyse this cultural shift in how one's problems and challenges ought to be interpreted and met. Paradoxically, in engaging in a programme of self-evaluation, the process of therapy reinforces the idea that people are unable to cope without intervention. He says:

> It is in fact through the capacity of the individual to manage the challenges of everyday life that insights may be gained into the workings of the self.

The verdict of therapeutic culture on this point is unambiguously clear. It casts serious doubts about the capacity of the self to manage new challenges and to cope with adversity. Individuals confronted with the ordinary troubles of life are now routinely advised to seek professional advice and counselling.

(Furedi, 2004, pp. 107–108)

Humanistic approaches place the individual at the centre (Rogers, 1951) and classical psychoanalytic approaches also locate meaning within the individual. Yet if this is the case, what or who is placed in the periphery?

Take a look at Figure 6.1. The partially obscured face turns away from the spectator: the woman stands, alone, wearing a certain expression. What do you think the artist is trying to convey? How do you react to this image? How might you describe this woman? If we assume that the woman is sad, or at least, pensive, what explanations could account for the woman's expression? If we were to see a client looking away from us,

Figure 6.1 *Sad Woman* by Lucy Littleford

their non-verbal expression suggesting the feeling of sadness, despair or even what we might tentatively associate with depression, what does that mean and how do we make sense of this? The answers to this question are surprisingly predictable. It is likely, for example, that we will think about the woman's circumstances, what she is feeling and whether she suffers from a clinical condition such as diagnosed depression, which may explain her state of mind. Other explanations would undoubtedly draw from a connection between the woman's cognition, or thoughts, about her mood and temperament. We may be interested in whether she has always felt like this or if something has occurred to prompt an emotional reaction. We may also have a view on her clothing and the draping of the scarf around her neck and the colour of blue.

In 'reading' the emotional state of the client, as social workers we are interested in what the woman herself told us as well as our interpretation of her non-verbal behaviours. As we discussed in Chapters 2 and 5, as social workers it is also vital to understand the filters through which we make our assessment of the client's situation. Yet there is another level of awareness that we ought to have. In making sense of client situations we are also influenced by the cultural conditions around the 'reading' of emotion. As discussed earlier, therapeutic discourse is prevalent and can serve to place the individual in a vacuum, away from the culture, society and community with which they interact.

Through the process of assessment, social workers will take into account our clients' narratives, their social relationships, any diagnoses and involvement with other organisations as well as other situations such as housing, income, employment and the social environments in which they live. In this sense, social work differs from other professions in that *social situatedness* is central to assessment. Considering the 'person in environment' contrasts other therapeutic approaches which solely look to an individual explanation for behaviour and affect. Not only is the 'person in environment' approach a core theoretical model in social work, it also reflects the value-base of the profession (Dybicz, 2015).

From the very first 'reading' of the image above, we somewhat 'unwittingly' employ particular theoretical lenses which shape our understandings. These influences are unknown to us unless we draw away from the individual and think about the social, political and historical forces which shape perception, as we discuss in Chapter 3, where we introduce social imaginaries and a sociological imagination. Further, the theoretical application to situations is important. For example, if we follow Furedi's thesis, which challenges the contemporary focus on 'therapy culture', we are encouraged to understand that sadness is just one expression in a range of human emotion and that individuals are able to develop resilience in the face of challenges. We might also think about his line, 'Individuals confronted with the ordinary troubles of life are now routinely advised to seek professional advice and counselling' and focus on his analysis that what happens now is different to what might have been the case in previous times.

In our present day, the focus of the individual – their cognition, emotional dimensions – is not accidental but rather is a result of the coming together of particular historical and social conditions. Many sociological theories point to historical developments which have had an impact on the ways in which we make sense of what is happening, both in our society and as individuals in that society. Giddens explains this:

> We might, of course, simply say that the search for self-identity is a modern problem, perhaps having its origins in Western individualism...The idea that each person has a unique character and special potentialities that may or may not be fulfilled is alien to pre-modern culture. In medieval Europe, lineage, gender, social status and other attributes relevant to identity were all relatively fixed. Transitions had to be made through the various stages of life, but these were governed by institutionalised processes and the individual's role in them was relatively passive.
>
> (Giddens, 1991, pp. 74–75)

The recent 'therapeutic turn' in society is an example of the focus on the individual. Reiff notes that '... a heavily remissive psychotherapy may become a permanent institutional fixture of modern culture – a kind of secular methodism for those who remain obstinately uncomfortable in their pleasures' (Reiff, 1966, pp. 204–205). Again, one need only look to popular culture to see the individualised landscape in which entertainment is shaped around self-improvement to see that the 'individual as project' (Giddens, 1991) is an enduring trope in society. Yet if social forces encourage a focus on individual action, how responsible are people for their actions? In turn, what might this suggest or imply for the role of social work, and the public expectation on social work?

This picks up on a central question in sociology – namely, what is the degree to which individual actions are made sense of through human agency? Or are individual actions embedded in social pressures and expectations? There is no clear answer and there is much debate around this issue, as we explore in this book and, in particular, in Chapter 5. As we note in earlier chapters we do not see the categories 'individual' and the 'social' as dichotomous. Individual issues must always be placed in a social context, as Mills argues. For the purposes of this chapter it is important to note that sociology reminds us that there are patterns to individual actions.

One of the most famous examples in sociology is Durkheim's study of suicide in which he analysed the role of society – and social conditions – to explain what is usually formulated as an individual 'problem'. If we think of suicide we often imagine it to be an individual problem. Instead, Durkheim looked for patterns in specific cultural settings to better understand who and why people decided to end their lives. Instead of seeing suicide as an individual, personal issue, he reoriented suicide as a social and cultural phenomenon. Drawing from data, Durkheim formulated a theoretical explanation for suicide which explained the relationship between the social and the individual and the resultant suicide rate.

Mills (1970) expounds on this relational dynamic by giving a particular example of job loss; a 'private pain' of unemployment cannot be just left with an individual but it is both this and a 'public trouble'. This is as salient now as when he was writing in the 1950s. At the time of writing this book many OECD industrialised countries are experiencing the loss of manufacturing industries and with it livelihoods and rippling out effects on communities. In South Wales in the United Kingdom, there are negotiations about the fate of the Tata steel plant based in Port Talbot. In Whyalla, South Australia, the town's largest employer, a steelmaker and iron ore mining company, was facing uncertainty and possible job losses. In both South Wales and South Australia, the implications for geographic and work-based communities from these changes are immense. Although in different hemispheres, what these workers and communities have in common is the intertwining of the local economic means of production and the construction of social and community life and identity. Industry closure and uncertainty about the security of jobs have profound impacts, not just on the workers themselves and their households and families, but the communities in which they are deeply embedded (Verity and Jolley, 2009).

Employing the relational perspective articulated by Mills acknowledges the circumstances for individual workers experiencing job loss, and what it will mean for their futures and well-being. We see beyond an individual 'private pain' but hold this together with a sense of the dynamic context of the changing nature of global capital and trade between nations. There is a complex dynamic which has many faces or dimensions: the faces of employees losing paid work; historical developments in state public policies and the capitalist market operations that set the conditions and environments in which these industry closures could occur. The sociologist Zygmunt Bauman writes of this state of affairs:

> There is a new asymmetry emerging between exterritorial nature of power and the continuing territoriality of the 'whole life' – which the now unanchored

power, able to move at short motive and without warning, is free to exploit and abandon the consequences of that exploitation.

(Bauman, 1998, p. 9)

There is also a futuristic aspect where these scenarios multiply as technology changes the nature of production, nature of work and types of work, and the place of human labour. Nanotechnology, the increased use of robots and advanced computer systems, drones, the cloud and other developments have a logical knock-on effect to change the nature of work and displace human labour, themes we raised in earlier chapters.

Think back over the last ten years and how digital technological change has impacted on the nature of workplaces and the roles people are employed for. With desktop computers, online systems and emails, workers in areas such as social work are performing multiple tasks that in previous times would have been the domain of administrative staff. We return to these matters within organisations that employ social workers in Chapter 8.

Think about the impacts of online shopping on the high street or shopping precincts. In some places there has been a visible change in the landscape as small shops close. In a 2016 report by the World Economic Forum, *The Future of Jobs*, these changes in capitalist production are being termed the 'fourth industrial revolution', with predictions of substantial job loss and need for new skills. The report's authors write about the consequence of new technologies for where work occurs, and this theme of time/space compression is one we return to in a later chapter:

The most significant driver of change – across all industries – is the changing nature of work itself. As new technologies make 'anytime, anywhere' work possible, companies are breaking up tasks in new ways, leading to a fragmentation of jobs across many industries. These effects are further compounded by the rise of mobile internet and cloud technology, enabling the rapid spread of internet-based service models.

(2016 https://www.weforum.org/press/2016/01/five-million-jobs-by-2020-the-real-challenge-of-the-fourth-industrial-revolution/).

We have now explored some of the ways in which sociology has used patterns of individual behaviour to critically examine it in terms of its social and cultural meanings. Not only is it important to understand the impacts and effects that phenomena have on individuals, but it is crucial to understand that individual experiences are socially patterned.

Exercise

➢ What are the ways in which we are 'tied' to other individuals? Think about your own social experiences of ties and bonds?

➢ What does it mean to speak of community?

➢ What are the ways in which social ties influence our decisions and experiences?

Social ties and bonds

In contemporary social work, we often point to the degree to which individuals are connected or disconnected from social ties, and these are variously described: 'community'; 'social bonds', 'social capital', 'social connections'; 'family and kin relationships'; 'friendships'; 'social isolation'. The concept of 'social isolation' links in with our understanding of what it means to be an individual in society and we now move on to consider in more detail what this might mean for social work practice. This type of social analysis marked out the work of early sociologists, in their investigations of social worlds and the consequence of spatial, economic and cultural change.

Tonnies (1957), a German sociologist, described two types of social relations and used them to contrast and explain how social links were evolving in this changing world; *Gemeinschaft* ('community') and *Gesellschaft* ('society'). *Gemeinschaft* described 'community' as social relations with habitual ties and established mores and norms. Tonnies argued these were more commonplace in a pre-industrial period, when people lived in closer spatial proximity and in smaller units sharing production and cultural practices. These bonds and ties both reflected and reinforced family, kin and clan relationships and lifestyles. Tonnies distinguishes this type of interdependency as 'community' with *Gesellschaft* relations emerging in the industrialised cities, where human connections are between independent actors. In this type of *Gesellschaft* social relationship, communal attachments and obligations fade into the background, even though there may be trace memories (Tonnies, 1957; Dunk West and Verity, 2013).

Durkheim (1972) took a different tack and was critical of Tonnies, both his romanticism of community life and his pessimism about 'societal social relations'. A critique of a romanticised 'community' imagination is well placed; it can be entangled with fantasy and myths, conservative objectives and stereotypes about human character and collective behaviour

(Bryson and Mowbray, 1981). Furthermore, Durkheim was critical of an inherent assumption that social relations in cities are not organic or natural. He writes they are just different:

> Beyond purely individual actions there is in our contemporary societies a type of collective activity which is just as natural as that of the less extended societies of former days. It constitutes a different type, but between the two species from the same genus, as diverse as they are, there is not a difference in their basic natures.
>
> (1972, p. 1198)

His own work in '... classifying the different species of social solidarity' (1984, p. 24) stemmed from an interest in the function of the division of labour within a society, the boundaries of self and society, social cohesion and integration. Durkheim developed the notions of 'organic' and 'mechanical' solidarity as describing key processes which form social glue, in other words as means of societal integration. Mechanical solidarity was evident when there is homogeneity between people and a low division of labour, or what he called 'solidarities by similarities'. Organic solidarity reflected the processes of interdependence in larger social systems marked by work diversification and differences.

A more contemporary lexicon is the language of social capital to explain an individual's social connectedness in a societal context. Pierre Bourdieu is a seminal writer in this tradition who developed a framework which holds together three types of capital: economic capital, cultural capital and social capital (1986). Each is a signifier of power relations and each can be transformed or exchanged for profit or economic gain. He extended the principles of the accumulation and exchange of economic capital to make visible other dimensions of power, value and exchange within a society. Cultural capital can be reflected in cultural sensibilities, 'cultural goods' and educational attainment (1986, p. 17). Of social capital, Bourdieu writes:

> Social capital is the aggregate of the actual or potential resources which are linked to possession of a durable network of more or less institutionalized relationships or mutual acquaintance and recognition – or in other words, to membership in a group – which provides its members with the backing of the collectively owned capital, a 'credential' which entitles them to credit, in the various senses of the word. These relationships may exist only in the practical state, in material and/or symbolic exchanges which help to maintain them. They may also be socially instituted and guaranteed by the application of a common name (the name of a family, a class, or a tribe or of a school, a party etc.) and by a whole set of instituting acts designed simultaneously to form

and inform those who undergo them; in this case, they are more or less really enacted and so maintained and reinforced, in exchanges.

(1986, p. 21)

One of the key and distinctive aspects of Bourdieu's notion of social capital is '... [t]he reproduction of social capital presupposes an unceasing effort of sociability, a continuous series of exchanges in which recognition is endlessly affirmed and reaffirmed' (1986, p. 22).

Let's apply some of this thinking to social work. In the first part of this chapter we have looked at the rise of an individualised culture where there is a focus on interpreting individual lives through the frame of individual meaning and responsibilities. Furedi identifies this as a feature of modernity, and his argument that we have an individualised culture in the modern epoch is based on a comparison to the situation in earlier historical times when this was not so widespread. But as social beings, we socially interact within cultures, communities, networks, workplaces in which this individualised culture, and the individual, is part. How these interconnections operate, what they signify and what they result in, are particularly pertinent questions for social workers to think about as we have our dual mission of the person in their environment and the micro and the macro to hold together.

Take a look at Figure 6.2. What do you think about when you see the collection of images? Unlike the individual portrait at the beginning of the chapter, these images are entitled 'Sad Women', suggesting a sadness that is shared by more than one person. We can also note another pattern: gender. Why would women in a society be portrayed as 'sad'? Is it

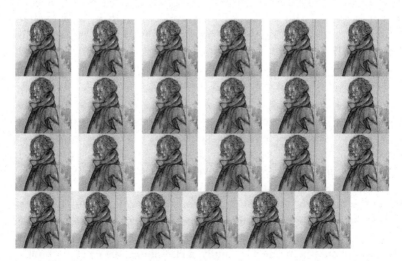

Figure 6.2 *Sad Women* by Lucy Littleford

something about the society that would point to this shared emotion? Or are these individual issues? Let's take the issue of gender and understand the social issues currently facing women. We know, for example, that women experience higher rates of domestic violence than their male counterparts. Why might this be so? When social workers see one woman who is unhappy or dissatisfied with her situation what role does gender play in the helping relationship?

Yet what is the relationship between the individual and society? Giddens argues that we have unprecedented choice in contemporary societies because of the movement away from traditional roles which were inflexible and deterministic and left little room for individuals to exert power to change. He argues that:

> In many pre-modern contexts, individuals (and humanity as a whole) were more powerless than they are in modern settings. People typically lived in smaller groups and communities; but smallness is not the same as power. In many small-group settings individuals were relatively powerless to alter or escape from their surrounding social circumstances. The hold of tradition, for example, was often more or less unchallengeable.
>
> (Giddens, 1991, p. 192)

If we consider Figure 6.2, we might start to think about gender and the ability or inability of the individual to shift or change their social circumstances. For this reason, the ability to exert power to change individual circumstances continues to be affected by the same categories of identity which persist throughout history. Issues related to one's class, culture or gender continue to influence the degree to which an individual has power to change their circumstances (Skeggs, 1997, 2004). The question then becomes: are we free to change circumstances or are we still bound by the 'chains' of tradition? The answer to the question is that both propositions can be seen as true. If we return to the issue of gender, there have been important historical developments which have impacted women's participation in social and economic life, such as the right for women to vote and their participation in the paid workforce. Yet figures relating to each of these issues remain somewhat bleak in modern times. Women are still underrepresented in political life with just over twenty per cent of women represented globally in parliament (UN Women) and women continuing to be paid lower than their male counterparts and unrepresented at higher levels of pay in the global workforce (https://www.wgea. gov.au/sites/default/files/20160428_International_gender_equality_statistics_factsheet.pdf).

One of the explanations for these seemingly contradictory messages is that we are living in 'complex' times. Urry argues that seeing the world in terms of divisions between say the individual and the society or micro and macro dimensions to experience are unhelpful dichotomies which are better served by using a 'profound "relationality"' (Urry, 2007a, p. 122) to examine and explain social phenomena. Urry examines the global nature of the contemporary world and:

> [I]n coupling together the 'global' and 'complexity', the aim is to show that the former comprises a set of emergent systems possessing properties and patterns that are often far from equilibrium. Complexity emphasizes that there are diverse networked time—space paths, that there are often massive disproportionalities between causes and effects, and that unpredictable and yet irreversible patterns seem to characterize all social and physical systems.
>
> (Urry, 2007a, pp. 7–8)

Urry and others note that some of the key features of our contemporary world have been brought about by rapid technological growth and that these changes have had an irreversible impact on a range of areas in social life, such as the ways in which we communicate and how we divide our leisure and work lives (Beck, 1992; Urry, 2007a, 2007b). This has challenged those who seek to make sense of the changes within disciplinary boundaries, as Beck notes:

> I feel strongly that we have to be imaginative yet disciplined if we are to break out of the iron cage of conventional and orthodox social sciences and politics. We need a new sociological imagination which is sensitive to the concrete paradoxes and challenges of reflexive modernity and which at the same time is thoughtful and strong enough to open up the walls of abstraction in which the academic routines are captured.
>
> (Beck, 1999, p. 134)

If we return to the focus of this chapter, to understand the individual in their social context and to think about social work, there are a range of sociologically driven theories which resonate with the practice and scholarship dimensions to social work. For example, if we consider that there have been rapid technological changes which have impacted upon the ways in which we relate to one another, the way we communicate in day-to-day life, for example, what might this mean for social work practice?

In respect to the implications for social work practice, in many countries, the impact of individualised culture can be seen all throughout public policies and the organisation of service delivery: rigid means testing for social security, mutual obligation policies, case management, individualised service delivery, individual payment plans, 'three strikes' you are imprisoned justice policies, are some examples. These policies lead to ways of working and thinking that have a structuring function, not just to structure the organisation of the social work, and what the social worker can and cannot do in practice, but the inherent discourses structure or frame a view of the individual and centre in this frame individual responsibility for the situations faced and what is to be done about them. As we note above with the example of the impact of digital technology on work and employability, the individual will be caught up in these fast-moving global changes with consequences that cannot be solely interpreted by a focus on human agency, or indeed the actions of a national government. Global dynamics in the workings of capitalism, and the actions of transnational bodies are also in the frame as shaping the direction of power relations.

Furthermore there is at work what Nussbaum writes about as adaptive preferences; in short, different groups have different expectations and will put up with things in varying degrees. She says:

> We are especially likely to encounter adaptive preferences when we are studying groups that have been persistent victims of discrimination, and who may as a result have internalized a conception of their own unequal worth. It is certain to be true when we are concerned with groups who have inadequate information about their situation, their options, and the surrounding society – as is frequently the case, for example, with women in developing countries.
>
> (1997, p. 283)

This relationship is a key strand of sociological theorising. For example, Marx wrote, 'Society does not consist of individuals, but expresses the sum of interrelations, the relations within which these individuals stand' (1978a, p. 247), and '... the human essence is no abstraction inherent in each single individual. In its reality it is the ensemble of social relations' (1978b, p. 145). We mentioned at the opening of this chapter the work of the sociologist Georg Simmel, who was particularly focused on thinking about social forms and individuals. He wrote:

> But the question of how society is possible must be understood in a still more fundamental sense. ... To be sure, consciousness of the abstract principle that he [sic] is forming society is not present in the individual. Nevertheless, each individual knows that the other is tied to him – however much this knowledge of the other as fellow sociate, this grasp of the whole complex as society, is usually realized on the basis of particular, concrete contents.
>
> (1971, p. 8)

In a world of complexity and unpredictability the social forms of life are changing, and, as they emerge, we too need to be shifting our views and ideas, so as social workers we can locate people in their social environment, and not just the environment we are familiar with or idealised social environment, for example a sentimental conceptualisation of 'community' (Plant, 1974; Bryson and Mowbray, 1981). As Simmel states, we will operate with day-to-day experiences of being in social interaction, whether we call this family, kin, community, friends, neighbours and some combination of all of these, as will the people we work with.

The use of the language of roots and rootlessness suggests a grounding or non-grounding in a physical space. With the emergence and embedding of digital technologies in world systems, there has been a rise in the language of networks for describing community and social relations through virtual connections and imagined communities. Time and space are important constructs here and we explore them more comprehensively in Chapter 7.

Conclusions

This chapter has examined the relationship between individuals and their social contexts. We have begun to explore how individual issues are socially patterned. We have outlined the 'therapeutic turn' in which reflexive processes have been popularised as 'normal' in our contemporary world. Understanding the patterns in social life and utilising sociological scholarship assists social workers to better understand the broader contexts in which they work. Social theory also encourages social workers to think more critically about the 'solutions' they come up with for clients and understanding broader shifts assists social workers to appreciate exceptions, innovations and adaptations in our clients' lives. The role that community plays in shaping our social world has also been examined in this chapter. Social workers are important change agents and interact with individuals, communities and groups: this legacy is important to continue as we face the challenges of late modern life.

Practising social work sociologically

Social work has a strong tradition of understanding individuals in their family, social and cultural frameworks. The use of Ecomaps (Hepworth, Rooney, Rooney and Strom-Gottfried, 2016) is an example of a practice which helps externalise and locate issues and connections between these different systems. It is therefore important that social workers continue to orient individuals within systems of support and communities rather than pathologising individuals. This is made difficult through contemporary policy in which we can see a re-orientation away from communities and more focused on individualised care and support. Whereas this can be helpful for some of the people with whom we work, it is nevertheless important to recognise the social ties that are important to wellbeing and people's sense of community. Working with individuals, groups and communities, sociological social work involves:

➤ Appreciation that humans are in social environments and are social actors

➤ Communities offer actors opportunities to come together and generate social change. Here the social worker's role is as a facilitator for positive, community-led social change

➤ Understanding the patterned and shared meanings and practices and looking for exceptions, innovations and resiliences

➤ Focusing at multi-levels through interventions.

7

Time and Space in Social Work

Time and space are concepts that are often underestimated in social work. In this chapter we explore what it means to be practising social work sociologically in relation to these concepts. In Ursula K. Le Guin's novel *The Dispossessed*, the following quote helps us understand how time and space create boundaries:

> *There was a wall. It did not look important. … Where it crossed the roadway, instead of having a gate it degenerated into mere geometry, a line, an idea of boundary. But the idea was real. It was important.*

So why are time and space important? These notions may seem somewhat philosophical yet it is important to understand these through a sociological lens. These concepts help to orient practice in the contemporary world. It is only in mapping some of the key issues in contemporary social work practice that we are able to think critically about the particular contexts in which social work takes place. Untangling the social, political, national and local practices and ways of working helps us to better inform and work positively with our clients/service users as well as take a structural approach to tackle inequalities. Using concepts from critical thinking, the roles that time and space play in shaping contemporary social work become less opaque and better understood. Social theory helps us draw away from and then back to day-to-day practice to better understand the social and historical significance of the challenges we face, rather as we did in the imaginary exercise on the International Space Station.

In this chapter we firstly explore what it means to be a citizen of the globe before moving on to better understand the role that the nation has in shaping our experiences. These examples of 'spaces' help to draw out, for example, how conceptualisations of humanness, and social connectedness are shifting and changing and are affected by global and local events and conditions. As Bourdieu writes, 'The social world is accumulated history' (1986, p. 15) and historical events have contributed to understanding the social world as connected across geographical and temporal boundaries. We therefore move on to examine the role that history has in shaping our meanings. Understanding social work practice as located in historical 'moments' helps to better inform and assist the people with whom we work. The chapter concludes with considering new forms of time and space and how these offer rich possibilities in the world of practice. First though, let's now move on to consider the global.

Time and space in contemporary life

Global space and time

The United Nations Declaration of Human Rights emerged following the horrific and devastating events brought about during the Second World War. A key architect of the Declaration, Eleonore Roosevelt, in speaking to the UN in a speech in December 1948, states:

> Man's [sic] desire for peace lies behind this declaration. The realization that the flagrant violation of human rights by Nazi and Fascist countries sowed the seeds of the last world war has supplied the impetus for the work which brings us to the moment of achievement here today.
>   (http://www.sojust.net/speeches/eleanor_roosevelt_adoption.html)

The development of the Declaration of Human Rights was prompted by the recognition that there are foundational principles which define what it means to live a life free from persecution, danger and violence. We noted in Chapter 4 that the IFSW is a social work grouping which sits across national borders and which shares a social imaginary. Similarly, the UN Declaration of Human Rights applies to citizens of the world, regardless of nationhood. The UN Declaration of Human Rights was formalised in late 1948 and outlines rights that are attached to individuals regardless of their nation state. In its preamble, this is articulated in the following way:

> Now, Therefore THE GENERAL ASSEMBLY proclaims THIS UNIVERSAL DECLARATION OF HUMAN RIGHTS as a common standard of achievement for all peoples and all nations, to the end that every individual and every organ of society, keeping this Declaration constantly in mind, shall strive by teaching and education to promote respect for these rights and freedoms and by progressive measures, national and international, to secure their universal and effective recognition and observance, both among the peoples of Member States themselves and among the peoples of territories under their jurisdiction.

We can see in this statement the emphasis on the 'common standard ... for all peoples and nations' hence the identification of Human Rights principles as 'universal'. Since the concept of human rights – that is, rights for *all humans* – came into public discourse, social work theory has drawn from this approach in the application of a human rights perspective. It is intrinsic to our collective imaginary. Whereas the development of a sociology of human rights is 'urgently' needed (Hynes et al., 2012) social work has integrated a human rights approach to social work theory and practice. Jim Ife argues that this perspective seeks to shift the power imbalance brought about though the attachment of theory and ethical codes to the social worker and, instead, use the universal approach a human rights perspective brings (Ife, 2008). In a sense, this shift asks us to reconsider the spatial placement and conceptualisation of theory and ethics. Consider Figure 7.1.

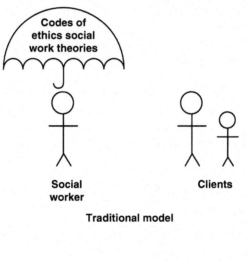

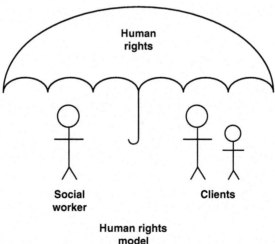

Figure 7.1 Spatial placement of human rights in social work

If we apply the notion of 'space' to better understand the advance of a human rights perspective we start to see the shift not only to whom theory and ethics are attached but also how a more literal application of the concept of space sees the disambiguation of the role of the nation and nationhood. Space cuts across human-made geographic and nationalistic boundaries. In this sense, space becomes a concept which is deliberately overwritten through the universal set of principles. Geographical space is therefore irrelevant when thinking about what conditions make for a human's safe and secure life and ability to thrive and live without fear, persecution or prejudice. Identity categories such as gender, age, culture, sexual identity, ability and so on are still important, but in this conceptualisation, human rights exist as a fundamental framework for understanding the rights of *humans*.

The establishment of the UN statement detailing the rights of all citizens – regardless of nation – is an important historical shift. If we consider the concept of 'time' in relation to human rights, these factors emerge:

➤ Human rights came about from a motivation to prevent past historical events in which people were persecuted, tortured and killed.

➤ Globalisation and the subsequent connectivity of people worldwide has enabled 24/7 technology-enabled communication

➤ Human rights continue to be adapted and re-used across different contexts (for example, in setting out children's rights): here the notion of time is important to point out the evolving of human rights approaches into the future.

Now that we have considered global space and time by using a human rights framework, we move on to consider how the concept of 'nation' impacts on our understanding of social issues.

Nation as space

At the same time as having a sense that nation-space can transcend a human rights approach, we also know that in social work practice it is important to recognise the national policy and legislative and cultural contexts in which the work takes place. This requires a dual focus: global and national space. Social workers can often readily recognise the influences that policy, legislation and organisations have in their day-to-day practices. In particular fields of practice – say child protection or safeguarding adults – legislation, regulations and policies are often at the forefront of practitioners' minds when decision-making occurs. We argue that it is also important to recognise the different geographical 'spaces' in which social issues occur. Not only is it vital for practitioners to see practice as taking place within the contexts of institutions and broader legislative frameworks, but the application of the concept of nation-space can help locate social problems and promote deeper thinking about the location in which practice takes place.

With a dual spatial mind-set we also hold the idea that in contemporary times we are linked beyond national borders, as has been theorised through the concept of globalisation. Globalisation scholars argue that the world has become more connected and complex as a result (Urry, 2005) and such a movement de-anchors individuals away from traditional social and interpersonal ties (Bauman, 1998), and opens national borders. Although there are compelling reasons to engage in the idea of a globalised community – such as the ways in which human rights are designed to cut across international borders as we have discussed – national (West, 2015), intentional and cooperative employment-based communities and national identities (Hurd and Dyer, 2017) continue to exist. An international lens can support us to better understand social issues and problems and the varied nation-based and international causes and responses to them. This is the international sensibility Alice Salomon and Jane Addams illustrated so well throughout their social work.

If we consider the ways in which nations respond to the social problem of drug and alcohol misuse, for example, we can see a picture emerge in which national and local legislative frameworks shape practice. A recent study into England's drug-use services, for example, found that interagency work and education about support services were vital for service delivery. Here, Weston argues that *integration* is key to successful service provision:

> ...to take multi-agency working to the level required to address the multiple needs presented by drug users, drug policy and commissioning arrangements need to focus on the integration of the drug treatment workforce into local community health and social care services. Only when such integration is achieved can a fully multidisciplinary approach to the treatment of drug dependency be realised.
>
> (Weston, 2016, p. 258)

In other European nations, the social issue of drug and alcohol misuse has been differently legislated, which has impacted on patterns of use and the ways in which those with drug-related issues are treated. For example, Portugal adopted a therapeutic response in favour of criminal justice provisions for people who had drug-related issues. This change has had a follow-on impact on the ways in which professionals work with people who misuse illicit drugs, as Laqueur describes below:

> The most dramatic change in Portugal after 2001 was not the legislation itself, nor any subsequent shifts in behavior with respect to drug use that followed. Instead, it was a change in the court system practices regarding the imposition of the criminal law for drug *trafficking*, despite the fact that such conduct remained and remains criminal. The number of arrests for trafficking changed little since passage of the decriminalization statute. However, there has been a significant decline in the number of convictions for trafficking, and an even steeper drop in prison sentences for drug trafficking. As a result, since 2001, the number of individuals incarcerated for criminal acts involving the sale, distribution, or production of drugs dropped by close to half.
>
> (Laqueur, 2015, p. 749)

It is important to recognise the ways in which small changes to legislative frameworks flow through to other areas of practice. Portugal sought to shift the response to illicit drug trade and use from one that was dominated by a legal framework to one which addressed people's needs more fully:

> What may be most significant about decriminalization in Portugal is not its prescriptive content, but what the law says about the normative valences that it both signaled and reinforced. The statute did not encompass a major change in legal sanctions. But it reflected and supported Portugal's evolving shift from a penal to a therapeutic approach to drug abuse and this, in turn, appears to have had a much broader impact on court practices.
>
> (Laqueur, 2015, p. 749)

The application of thinking about nation-space to social problems can assist social workers in the 'doing' of the work, particularly given the dominance that policy and legislation have in contemporary practice. The national context, we argue, remains an important starting point to better understand how and why issues become social problems. This kind of thinking provides the mechanism to critically think and challenge systems which thwart social justice-oriented practice (Figure 7.2).

Figure 7.2 is aimed to conceptualise social problems through the lens of the nation. National legislation, policy, social attitudes and organisational funding and arrangements all impact on the way in which a social issue is understood – including by social workers. In order to distance ourselves from our everyday experiences – after all, we are all situated in national contexts – it can be useful to think through the ways in which the national identity impacts on our assumptions, and the differing ways in which nations narrate and respond to social issues. Better understanding international research about a social issue, for example, and the

- **How is the social issue defined nationally?**

- **How has the nation defined the issue now and in the past and into the future?**

- **How do other nations treat the social issue?**

- **How is practice impacted through the national context?**

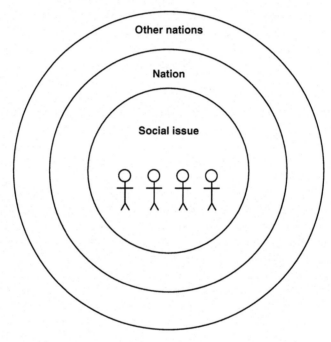

Figure 7.2   Thinking about nation

contexts within which shifts in attitudes in other nations occur, promote informed practice. Moving away from the personal or taken-for-granted assumptions about a particular issue ultimately assists social workers to better advocate for social change, to remain informed about international movements and shifts and to work with clients or service users. We now move on to consider the ways in which time – as historically constructed – establishes particular assumptions about social issues.

Historical perspectives

It is fairly easy to see how the concept of time relates to understanding history: time is a concept situated in the punctuated notions of the past, present and future. In Chapter 2 we outlined key historical figures in the development of social work. These women practised in geographically diverse contexts, in their times, and yet they shared some common characteristics such as the dedication to address particular forms of social disadvantage and inequalities. When we think of 'history' sometimes it is easy to forget that we are historically situated. Right now, we are at a particular point in history. We make history in an ongoing way. The day-to-day immersion in social life can make it difficult to retain an overarching historical perspective about particular social issues. Social workers often work 'on the ground' with people and it can be easy to forget the historical situatedness of practice. As we saw in the previous section about nation-based assumptions, so are we often too engaged in the everyday to lift the lens upwards to a more macro historical perspective. Giddens notes that:

> The study of day-to-day life is integral to analysis of the reproduction of institutionalized practices. Day-to-day life is bound up with the repetitive character of reversible time – with paths raced through time-space ...
>
> (Giddens, 1984, p. 282)

The study of day-to-day life means, somewhat paradoxically, drawing away from the mundane practices of daily interactions, assumptions and the 'overlooked norm' (Gardiner, 2004, p. 229). We argue that the historical lens is an important one to apply to better understand social issues and their associated 'norms'. Let's take a look at some examples of recent concepts that are relevant to contemporary social life:

➤ Risk

➤ Anxiety

➤ Depression

➤ Stress

➤ Mindfulness

➤ Addiction

➤ Work/life balance

➤ Trauma

➤ Body image

➤ Self-esteem

➤ Alternative facts

If we look at these concepts using an historical lens, it can assist in conceptualising how and why particular issues have become prevalent in the contemporary world. That is not to say that these issues are 'merely socially constructed': this is important to understand. Understanding how and why something is constructed does not in any way undermine the reality of people's lived experience. People new to the idea of social constructionism can assume that by recognising that something is socially constructed means that it is unimportant or easy to change, just by thinking differently. This cannot be further from the truth. Instead, social constructionism recognises the broader social, historical and political influences on social life and the meanings we hold.

The ways in which particular issues come to the fore in particular historical times are important to understand in order for social workers to be able to better conceptualise and understand issues relevant to practice and social work theory and balance this knowledge with other approaches such as those informed by psychological theories. University education emphasises that the application of a critical thinking lens helps to interrogate the taken-for-granted meanings we hold (Stupple et al., 2017). Questions which characterise critical reflections include the following 'thinking points' in which X represents a social issue (such as those listed above), and the questions are the type of 'critical thinking' exercises used with students (Kuhn, 1999).

> Who benefits or profits from X?

> Who suffers because of X?

> When did X become better known?

> How do other cultures conceptualise X? Why are there differences?

> What is the future of X?

> What role does power play in the creation of X?

> To whom is power available through X? Legislators? Policy makers?

> How could X be reimagined?

> What knowledge of X might help social workers and their clients/ service users?

Let's now take a look at something topical and seemingly straightforward: sex addiction. If we turn to popular media, reports on celebrity infidelity often reinforce the idea that we can become 'addicted' to sex. This concept – that we can be 'addicted' to sexual behaviour – is backed up through scholarship and research. So does that mean it's 'true'? Or can we assume that it's 'true' for everyone? The approach taken in this book is to encourage critical thinking and drawing from sociological perspectives can assist in this process.

Sex addiction, at face value, seems to be, at the very least, a legitimate concern to many and potentially cause of a great deal of distress and difficulty for its sufferers. Yet what is meant by sex addiction? As with any form of addiction, the importance of the distress it causes the person or others close to them is foremost:

> The shift from a normal passion to addiction may be barely perceivable because dependence and need for the other are present in love passion. Addiction would be defined as the stage where desire becomes a compulsive need, when suffering replaces pleasure, when one persists in the relationship despite knowledge of adverse consequences (including humiliation and shame).
>
> (Reynaud et al., 2010, p. 263)

This definition makes sense, particularly in relation to other kinds of addictions such as drug and alcohol misuse. However, if we apply an historical lens to better understand how sex became associated with 'addiction' we can see that the categorisation of sexuality has strong historical ties. Those defining problematic sexuality primarily come from psychiatry, which is a profession with an idiosyncratic approach:

> Investigating the history of how and why psychiatrists, sexologists, and other mental health professionals delineated sexual pathology from normal sexuality and/or criminal behavior, current historians have to engage with 19th- and 20th-century theories about the etiology, diagnosis, classification, and treatment of sexual deviance.
>
> (De Block and Adriaens, 2013, p. 294)

Interestingly, addiction to sex, or hypersexual disorder, is not specifically listed in the most current American Psychiatric Association's Diagnostic and Statistical Manual of Mental Disorders – the DSM (Krueger, 2016); however, it was listed in previous editions such as the DSM-II:

> As to the perversions, one of the minor novelties of DSM-II was the introduction of an explicit list of eight sexual deviations: homosexuality, fetishism, pedophilia [sic], transvestism, exhibitionism, voyeurism, sadism, and masochism.
>
> (De Block and Adriaens, 2013, p. 286)

The enduring power of the DSM to identify and categorise normal and abnormal behaviour cannot be underestimated. Similarly, social problems such as teenage pregnancy need to be seen as constitutive through the interaction of broader social, political and moral frameworks (Dunk-West, 2013a). Recent research in the United Kingdom found that social workers are influenced by broader social inequalities such as homophobia (Schaub et al., 2016). Social scientists and activists have played a role in challenging previously categorised so-called sexual pathologies, such as homosexuality:

> In the bulk of the historical literature about psychiatry's dealing with deviant sexuality, homosexuality has received the lion's share of the attention. Exhibitionism, sadism, fetishism, and other sexual deviations or paraphilias are only marginally touched on. The main reason for this discrepancy is that, historically, psychiatrists themselves have always been short of decent data about deviations other than homosexuality – partly because they are supposedly less common than homosexuality, and partly because the gay activist lobby has always been quite powerful. Thus, homosexuality has played an important part in the history of psychiatry, culminating in the 1974 APA referendum and the subsequent removal of homosexuality from the DSM. The controversy over homosexuality forced the APA to come up with a definition of mental disorder in DSM-III, which has since served as a touchstone to include or exclude many other disease categories. Yet somewhat ironically, many of the sexual deviations are still listed as mental disorders in recent editions of the manual.
>
> (De Block and Adriaens, 2013, pp. 293–294)

The removal of homosexuality as a categorised mental illness was relatively recent, historically speaking. Understanding the historical situatedness of social issues is therefore important when considering sexuality. Plummer notes that histories intersect when thinking about sexuality:

> Our social sexual worlds always lie at the intersections of our generations (along with other locations such as class, gender, nation and ethnicity). All sexualities dangle from an age perspective. They are situated in age standpoints. At any moment of thinking about the sexual, we will usually find at least five generations helping shape that moment. And these are just the living generations – to this there will also be the legions of dead generations, whose ghosts may still be heard speaking past sexual stories.
>
> (Plummer, 2010, p. 165)

Now that we have explored the additional meanings and insights that the application of an historical lens brings, we move on to consider the present 'time'. Time can constrain social work practice and here we consider some of the contemporary manifestations of 'time' in relation to social work.

Time as a constraint to social work practice

We live in a world in which information is largely available via technology. Yet how do we navigate knowledge in the new era of web 2.0: the interactive and democratised space that the internet provides? Han notes that because of the co-existence of technological advance and connectivity, information and knowledge are newly imagined:

> ... to grieve the de-coupling of knowledge and freedom may require such a compensatory supplement, it may also be that knowledge has transformed not simply because of clear failures it has had in coming through its promises of freedom and equality under the umbrella of humanity, but also because of the convergence of media technologies and humans, making knowledge no longer useful as perhaps the concept of 'information' is.
>
> (Han, 2010, p. 211)

Similarly, the notion of time has been theorised to have 'sped up' (Lash, 2001) because of the advance of communicative technology. Again, this raises questions about the ways in which social work services are arranged and experienced by both the practitioner and the people with whom they work.

Social workers must be able to access knowledge such as through research-informed approaches and they are also required to navigate deadlines and report writing. Here, time and space can compromise the quality of the work. Formal reviews into child protection often cite 'time-pressures' as impacting on the work. Such constraints on the time that workers are able to spend with clients have been found to impact on a social worker's ability to be 'free' to think through practice decisions (see Munro, 2011). In this way, time is depicted as a constraint to quality practice.

Other examples of time as a limiting factor in quality social work practice come from the organisational context. Social work students are often taught communication skills in the context of one-to-one work. This can set up an expectation of what social work entails in an agency or organisational setting. The expectation for many students entering their placement is that they will see clients for a set period of time, such as in the office, and direct a formal process whereby information from the client is assessed to identify needs and anticipate services relevant to those identified needs. Recent research, however, has found that social workers' interactions occur in 'non traditional spaces' (Saltiel, 2015) which are under-theorised and researched (Ferguson, 2011). This has an impact on the ways in which time is experienced.

For example, limited contact with clients or service users can seem somewhat different to the ways in which social work practice is taught in the classroom. Contacting a client over the telephone or taking a client to an appointment are examples of the 'non traditional spaces' in which social workers can engage and develop positive working relationships with the people with whom they work. These opportunities are shorter in time, usually brief, and the social work role can be easily seen as secondary to the purpose of the interaction.

Rather than seeing the work as constrained by time, social theories can assist in understanding new and creative ways that traditional models of social work have been transformed into non-traditional spaces (Ferguson, 2008). For example, car journeys can be seen as 'therapeutic opportunities' in which the counselling room is replaced with conversations during a somewhat mundane car ride (Ferguson, 2009). Home visits must be seen as rich opportunities for social workers to better understand, observe and interact with clients (Ferguson, 2011).

Given that these new conceptualisations of time and space differ from traditional models of social work, it is useful to reflect on these shifts. Here we offer a reflexive tool so that the new spaces and times that interactions occur can be realised (Table 7.1).

Conclusions

In this chapter we have explored the meanings that social theories bring to considerations of the concepts of time and space. We have examined the nationhood and global identity to better understand how these contexts shape our experiences. We have also examined how 'time' is helpful in an historical context since it is only through the interaction of social, political and economic forces that issues become prevalent in particular historical epochs. Finally, we explored new possibilities for the ways in which time and space are experienced and understood in contemporary social work practice.

TRADITIONAL SPACES	MY SPACES	RICHNESS/POSSIBILITIES
Counselling room		
Telephone		
Intake processes		
Office-based interactions		
Home visits		

Table 7.1   Spatial Placement of Human Rights in Social Work

Practising social work sociologically

Time and space are important to social work practice. Space has been explored in this chapter in relation to the nation, to the global and to the local contexts of practice. We have examined time in relation to the rise of technology and the impacts of communicative technologies on our sense of time. Time pressures in social work are enduring issues. Some of the antidotes to feeling that there is not enough time is to reconceptualise the 'non-formal' interactions we have with clients as important to building a helping relationship and considering these opportunities as those in which social work takes place. Time is also important to the broader ways in which social problems are conceptualised: history shows us that particular issues or social problems are related to the conditions of the social and cultural contexts in which they emerge. Understanding the role of time and space involves practising social work sociologically by:

➤ Identifying and recognising the historical events which influence contemporary social work practice and being able to engage with the people with whom we work about how this impacts on their day-to-day lives

➤ Appreciating and naming the new and innovative ways that time and space have been reconceptualised in contemporary social work practice and utilising new kinds of 'rich practice'

➤ Looking to nations to better understand how legal, ethical and social conditions understand, name and address social inequalities

➤ Translate meanings from global perspectives which shift relations of power between the practitioner and people with whom we work.

8

Organisations and Sociological Social Work

Introduction

A theme central to this book is the value of theoretical reference points which are strongly aligned with both the interpersonal dimension of social work and the political and socio-economic conditions within which social work is located. With this in mind, our attention in this chapter moves to the organisational contexts of social work practice. The challenges created by evolving managerialist and economic rationalist discourses and practices, coupled with variants of risk management and 'austerity' policies, run deep (Dominelli, 1997; Ife, 1997; Crimeen and Wilson, 1997; Froggett, 2002; Ferguson and Lavalette, 2013). In some contexts it is not unusual for social workers to work within an ever-narrowing frame of reference (Ferguson and Lavalette, 2013). 'Risk-averse' organisational systems and cultures also have impacted on social work practice in ways that are limiting (Dunk-West and Verity, 2013). These practices have deep implications for what takes place in organisations. They require a means to '...interpret and navigate the tensions between organisational remit and social work role and the emotions this will generate' (Dunk-West and Verity, 2013, p. 49).

Eldridge and Crombie published a book in 1974 on the sociology of organisations, in which they trace key ideas from the classical sociologists. Eldridge and Crombie (1974, p. 21) demonstrate how the concepts we use about organisations can direct how we proceed to explore them. They cite Talcott Parsons (1960), who identified organisations as entities '... deliberately constructed and reconstructed to seek specific goals or values' (Eldridge and Crombie, 1974, p. 23). Organisations are not to be regarded as fixed in stone but are better seen as relations and practices that are organised for a reason. Importantly, these relations, practices and ends can and do shift; in other words, they are dynamic. Eldridge and Crombie also quote Weber, who described an organisation as '[a] social relationship which is either closed or limits the admission of outsiders [and whose] regulations are enforced by specific individuals' (Eldridge and Crombie, 1974, p. 26). Organisations as a 'structured set of social relationships', driven by a 'purpose' and 'bounded', are some of the key elements we can extract from this definition. There are other ways to explore workplaces. We might follow the ideas of Bourdieu (2002) and explore them using his concepts of 'fields' or 'spaces of relations'; hone in on organisational structures and dynamics (Mohr, 2006) or organisational cultures and change (Czarniawska-Joerges, 1992; Martin, 2002).

In short, there are many ways of conceptualising and understanding organisations, and this complexity can be daunting (Eldridge and Crombie, 1974). A number of authors make use of the Harry Potter series in their elaborations on reflective practice, in particular the pensieve (e.g., Verity, 2003; Moon, 2004; Stevens and Boladeras, 2010; Gustar, 2014; Hargreaves, 2016). For example, Jennifer Moon (2004, p. 181), in her comprehensive work, uses Dumbledore's pensieve to evocatively draw together a rich seam of ideas about reflection. J. K. Rowling's Harry Potter novel *The Goblet of Fire* explains this wonderful invention of a pensieve. In a captivating scene, the wizard headmaster Dumbledore's thoughts leave his mind and stream into his pensieve. As Dumbledore explains to Harry Potter:

> **Dumbledore**: "I use the Pensieve. One simply siphons the excess thoughts from one's mind, pours them into the basin, and examines them at one's leisure. It becomes easier to spot patterns and links, you understand, when they are in this form."
>
> **Harry**: "You mean... that stuff's your thoughts?"
>
> **Dumbledore**: "Certainly."
>
> (Albus Dumbledore to Harry Potter, *Goblet of Fire*, 2000)

Following Moon's (2004) creative lead, we suggest that reflecting on the simultaneously bounded and shifting entities known as 'organisations', mindful of contested definitions, competing analytical pathways and the richness of experience, is going to require a pensieve, much like Dumbledore's device. There is a wisdom in Rowling's creation of a pensieve. This 'stuff', as Harry calls Dumbledore's 'thoughts', is more than a stream of consciousness; rather, the pensieve places thoughts in context. Gareth Morgan's work on organisational metaphors is one way to construct such a thinking device, and we now turn to his ideas as a framework for our discussion about the organisational settings of social work practice.

Gareth Morgan's organisational metaphors

As we note earlier, our approach in this chapter is to explore social work and organisations and we do so using Gareth Morgan's organisational metaphors as an analytical framework (1986, 1993, 2006). Writing from the field of management and organisational theory, Morgan developed a method for 'reading' and imagining organisations using metaphors which he set out in his reprinted book *Images of Organization* (1986, 2006). He calls this process 'Imaginization':

> ... a means whereby people in everyday situations can explore and challenge their taken-for-granted assumptions while opening up new avenues for understanding and action.
>
> (1993, p. xxix)

Morgan (1986, 2006) compiled eight organisational metaphors from his detailed analysis of historical ideas and theories about organisations across the fields of sociology, organisational studies and management. He terms these eight organisational metaphors as follows: organisations as 'organisms', organisations as 'machines', organisations as 'brain', organisations as 'psychic prison', organisations as 'culture', organisations as 'political system', organisations as 'change and flux' and organisations as 'instruments of domination'.

He is not advising a hierarchy within this list of eight metaphors, or a set way to 'read' organisations (2006, pp. 4–8). Rather, his approach is a structured and creative way to take some time to look, from different 'angles', at organisations in a process of deep, deep and deeper reflective practice. Metaphors are what Morgan calls '... understanding the unknown through the known' (Oswick and Grant, 2016, p. 10). Think of it as a way to engender the habit of imagination that C. Wright Mills was writing about and which we discussed in Chapter 4. Morgan (1996, p. 238), commenting on this work, writes:

> Superficially, *Images of Organization* presents eight metaphorical views of organization, analysing the domain of organizational theory to make its point. But its real power, and this I think is one of the major reasons why it has been so influential, rests in the fact that each metaphorical frame has the effect of deconstructing the others. ... Organizations are successively examined as

machines, organisms, brains, cultures, and so on, without asserting that they are ultimately any of these things.

This approach of using metaphors to think about or 'read' organisations has 'generative capacities'; in other words, we can 'generate insights and knowledge' in the process of thinking metaphorically (Grant and Oswick, 1996, p. 2; Morgan, 2006, p. 6). Lopez writes about metaphors with this transformative ability, where we think beyond the metaphor to something else:

> This metaphorical operation can be conceptualised as a 'catalyst' because in the process of producing new concepts, meanings and theoretical strategies, the initial connections with the domain from which the metaphor was drawn are severed.
>
> (2003, p. 16)

Importantly, metaphors are not truths and as such generate what Morgan (2006, p. 4) calls 'one-sided insights'.

Morgan's work is the organising logic in this chapter. We suggest his metaphorical approach is an incisive way for social workers to sharpen awareness of the dynamics and practices at work in organisations; not only positive dynamics that enhance effective social work practice, but just as important those that reinforce certain power relations and which we need to see if we are going to be able to do something about these. We are particularly mindful of the personal impact of practice in neo-liberal shaped organisations and, following a tradition of consciousness raising and resistance, the empowering nature of knowledge and understanding (Lee, 1994; Dominelli, 1997; Ferguson and Lavalette, 2013). This awareness can be a supportive 'cloak of curiosity' to wear, to hold close and create a boundary between systemic pressures and the worker's commitment to social work values. Grant and Oswick (1996, p. 3) call the use of metaphors as '... important to the advancement of knowledge and understanding'.

Exercise – Thinking about organisations that you have been part of

Think reflexively about your time in organisations, either in social work positions or through community development or voluntary work.

What are some of your earliest memories of working in an organisation?

What stand out as some key changes over time?

Using Morgan's organisational metaphors to think about social work and organisations

In the following discussion we present a short synopsis of just four of the organisational metaphors that Morgan (1986, 2006) has assembled and described: organisations as 'machines', 'organisms', 'brains' and 'instruments of domination'. These four are chosen to illustrate the usefulness of what Grant and Oswick (1996, p. 214) call Morgan's 'unique' approach. Throughout our discussion we follow a pattern. We first overview how Morgan describes this metaphor in the context of his sociological and historical investigation of organisational theories and metaphors, and then use our imaginations and experience to explore them in relation to social work and organisations.

For more detailed information on Morgan's thinking and metaphors we have included a number of his books in the reference list. You might also want to think about his other four metaphors of organisations that we do not include: the organisation as 'psychic prison', 'culture', 'political system', and 'change and flux'. We conclude each of the four sections with reflection questions. We are purposefully using the expression 'social work and organisations' rather than talking about 'social work organisations', as there will be social workers who work in organisations that fulfil functions beyond social work. For example, social workers will be part of a multi-disciplinary workforce in hospital settings and local authorities. There will also be organisations where the main staff group is social work.

Morgan's metaphor: organisation as 'machines'

Morgan begins his work with a well-used metaphor in the field of organisational studies and management, that of 'organisation as machine'. The familiar subject is a machine from which to creatively stretch to think about organisations. Morgan (2006, pp. 11–22) situates this way of viewing and running organisations in a historical context, canvassing military and industrial developments and theories. For instance, he highlights the influence of Frederick Taylor, the architect of 'The Principles of Scientific Management' published in 1911 (Morgan, 2006, pp. 22–26). In Taylor's model, the *organisation* works best to achieve its goals if there are clear scientific and rational principles used in planning and production, management and the allocation of roles throughout the organisation. Taylor created measures to both count the time taken to perform tasks with a view to increasing production rates and gather information about performance and outputs (Morgan, 2006).

As Morgan notes, Taylor's model lives on. There is no shortage of everyday examples of these machine-like practices in contemporary management and organisational behaviour. Morgan (2006, pp. 23–24) gives examples of fast-food chains (e.g., MacDonald's), which operate to a rational and technical template and where the workers do their part according to instructions developed by the organisational leaders. He writes, 'All the "thinking" is done by the managers and designers, leaving all the "doing" to the employees' (Morgan, 2006, p. 23).

Social work and organisations: a machine?

Turning to think about organisations that employ social workers, if we use this metaphor of an organisation as 'machine' what might come to mind is 'top-down' government funding specifications or regulations that set out what a service delivery system should do, together with performance indicators to report against and timeframes in which outcomes are to be achieved. Following Morgan, the 'thinking about what is required' is done elsewhere; in practice, it can be difficult to bring in local variation, contextual relevance and values (Ferguson and Lavalette, 2013). We have discussed these matters in previous chapters, and you will have examples from your own practice. The trend for the development of national data sets and performance measures that 'cascade down' is a concrete example. Neo-liberal ideas and a strengthening of a 'neo-liberal state' where public policies operate in alignment to principles and workings of liberal competitive markets have been one of the drivers of these developments (Williams, 1999; Harvey, 2005; Wacquant, 2010). David Harvey calls this an '...extension of market transactions using Deregulation, privatisation, and withdrawal of the state from many areas of social provision' (2005, p. 3).

Our mind's eye can also be drawn inward to the collection of data and performance measures within the organisation, or to requirements of how work will proceed through certain predesigned stages. In some settings, work is time prescribed so there may be time limits on work with clients or on the duration of community development or programmes, perhaps as set in funding conditions. These practices will look different across organisations where social workers are located. For example, social work in hospitals, local authorities and smaller third-sector organisations will each have their own ways of doing things and be part of distinct systems with their language and dominant practices. Risk management is another example of these technical and rational principles in practice, where there is a systematic and supposedly 'objective' way to define, measure and deal with risks (Verity, 2005). Using this metaphor, what comes to your mind?

At this stage you might be thinking of the criticisms or 'distortions' of approaching organisations as if they are machines, which is precisely what Morgan's process of 'imaginization' encourages. We have to also ask how an organisation is not a machine. Morgan writes that machines are 'dehumanizing' and do not take into consideration human interrelations and emotions, power dynamics and the unpredictability of everyday life (2006, p. 30). These human factors are at the centre of social work practice, what Clare Britton Winnicott articulates as '... *the common humanity that binds us and our clients together*' (2004, Chapter 9, Loc 4271). Planning and running an organisation as a machine leaves little room for the organisation to be 'heart filled' (Andrews, 2017), adaptive and with capacity to respond to diverse human experiences. Morgan writes that mechanistic approaches '... can result in mindless and unquestioning bureaucracy' (2006, p. 28). Social work is familiar with this situation.

Exercise – Imagining organisations which employ social workers as a machine

Think about your employing organisation where you work as a social worker, or where you are doing your social work placement, as a machine. What comes to mind?

What are some examples of 'machine-like thinking' in your organisation?

What are examples of 'machine-like practices' in your organisation?

What are the limits of this metaphor for social work practice in your organisation?

Morgan's metaphor: organisation as 'organism'

Let's turn to another one of Morgan's images of organisations, namely as 'organisms'. Biological metaphors are frequently used in sociological theorising, for example in the work of classical sociologist Emile Durkheim (Lukes, 1973; Morgan, 2006), and we have our own examples in social work literature. Morgan asks us to think, in his words, '... about organisations as if they were organisms' (2006, p. 33). Where would our mind turn? Morgan, from his historical analysis of ideas in organisational theory and practice, uses this metaphor to draw out some key similarities. We briefly summarise his main points before turning to our application of this metaphor to social work and organisations.

Organisations are diverse in structure, what Morgan calls the 'variety of the species' (2006, p. 49). Just as there are seagulls, owls, humans and gorillas, there is a wide spread of organisational form, reflecting what they do and how they interact in their environment. Morgan (2006, pp. 49–51), with reference to organisational theorists such as Mintzberg, Handy and Quinn, lists some of these 'species': 'simple organisations', 'bureaucratic structures', 'cluster organisations', 'virtual organisations' and so on. Organisations will go through cycles of development and stages of varying strength and vitality, and like organisms have internal systems of interconnected parts that work in alignment to ensure survival (Morgan, 2006).

Organisms are not isolated but exist within a wider context or eco-system, and as Morgan writes they have a boundary that is responsive to external conditions. He states, 'A living organism, organization, or social group is a fully open system' (2006, p. 40). Moreover, the focus is on maintaining a 'steady state' (Morgan, 2006, p. 40) in relation to the external environment; adaptation and survival is dependent on this rela-tionship. The word 'open' is important and indicates a boundary that is permeable to external conditions and factors, and where there is contact with others in the ecosystem. In summary, Morgan has drawn out the fol-lowing: organisations like organisms have 'open systems'; the capacity to adapt to the outside context; are diverse; have stages of 'development and health' over time; and are part of an ecology (2006, p. 34).

Social work and organisations: an organism?

Using biological metaphors is also not unfamiliar in social work. In social work and ecological theories there is a language of nested systems (micro, meso, macro domains), and systems and integrative thinking. The *Life Model of Social Work* by Germain and Gitterman, published in 1980, is an example of a social work model where the organising logic for social work practice is based on awareness of cycles of interdependence between dynamic natural, economic and social worlds, and within social worlds. Social work recognises interconnections and holism. As Germain and Gitterman explain:

> The ecological perspective presents our view that human needs and problems are generated by the transactions between people and their environments.
>
> (1980, p. 1)

But let's think about organisations and social work using this metaphor. There is a range of heterogeneous organisations that employ social work-ers, as we mentioned earlier. These vary in what they do and why, the people they work with and source of funds (i.e., government, private sector, charitable sources). They will also vary in the organisational structure. Some may be smaller organisations with flatter decision-making structures or community management, and others larger and bureaucratic with the attendant features. There will also be diversity in the client group, practice methods, and other features which will be determined by history and the social and cultural context (Dunk West and Verity, 2013). Think about organisations you know. How would you describe them?

We might also zoom in on the components within organisations and how they are organised and interconnected. For example, within organisations social workers will play different roles, and depending on this role they might work according to different processes and be part of distinct cultures. As well, organisations have colours, sounds, smells and a feel, which will tell something of the organisational culture. In her work on organisational culture, Martin writes:

> Manifestations of culture include rituals, stories, humour, jargon, physical arrangements, and formal structures and policies, as well as informal norms and practices.
>
> (Martin, 2002, p. 55)

A further point made by Morgan (2006) is that organisms survive if they are 'healthy', and the environment in which they live is healthy. Think about what it takes to keep a pond clean and remove the toxic algae so fish and other pond inhabitants stay alive. A parallel in organisations where social work services are based is to work for healthy relational cultures that value and respect the human beings who come into contact with the organisation; respect for people in not defining them only by the dominant human service language and respect expressed in physical spaces (waiting areas, offices, meeting rooms, use of colour, and signs of inclusive and appropriate welcome). For the employees, think of their work satisfaction and value, and how this is best supported (Morgan, 2006, p. 36).

As well as internal activity and patterns of power and authority, organisations where social workers are located are within a delivery system in a social, political and economic context. They are not isolated and work by and large in systems which are interconnected, as models of ecological social work make clear. Social workers work with people, families, communities, groups and issues that are interconnected. The external context is a site of social work practice, for what Jones and May call understandings about the dynamic contexts in which people live and the 'focus of intervention' (Jones and May, 1992). However, increasingly across many parts of the world, these delivery systems are framed by guidelines and policies that are developed centrally, using neo-liberal logic, with implications for the nature of openness and for external engagement. An outcome of managerialist and economic rationalist discourses and practices in human services is competition amongst social service agencies for limited funds; the antithesis of such openness as competition encourages keeping things close and reducing open communication (Dunk West and Verity, 2013).

But, whilst useful to think this way, as Morgan makes clear there are critiques of biological analogies and limits to their usefulness (Morgan, 2006). We can lose sight of non-biological dynamics such as power relations including structural power and our own personal agency, organisational culture and the choices that are made or not made by organisational leaders. Morgan (2006) makes clear that organisations are not neutral as social units. For example to think about 'movement to equilibrium', which for an organism is the movement to reach a state of balance, is misleading in understanding organisations in the context of social work.

There are circumstances when a 'steady state' is a status quo that might perpetuate an ethically untenable or unjust situation. It may be that dominant practices within an organisation reinforce class-, race-, gender- or sexuality-based interests; they might be taken for granted as the norm. Social workers are called upon to challenge such equilibriums. Furthermore, to adapt to the external environment (in our current context where neo-liberal ideas are dominant) might ensure the survival of the organisation, but at what cost if this means a trade-off with its history, core values and ethics and overriding purpose. Finally, and this applies to all the metaphors we are considering in this chapter, how we read organisations as 'organisms' will reflect social work values, experiences and expectations about organisational practices and also world views.

Exercise – Imagining organisations which employ social workers as an organism

Think about your employing organisation, or where you are doing or did your placement, as an organism. What sort of organism is in your mind?

How does your organisation gather intelligence about the external context?

How does it stay 'healthy'?

Where are the limits of thinking about organisations as organisms?

Morgan's metaphor: organisation as 'brain'

The third metaphor we overview is what Morgan has imagined as the organisation as a 'brain'. At first glance it might seem peculiar to think about organisations this way. But what Morgan communicates are the ways in which the brain functions as the human's 'information processing system', regulator and controller (2006, p. 71). This includes regulating our internal biological systems, emotions, cognition and development. Morgan describes how organisations, like brains, have interconnected learning and knowledge-processing functions. Organisational learning and communication are two angles Morgan explores in using this metaphor.

We can see some of the complexities of the brain in the expanding knowledge generated through neuroscientific research, especially about the extent of the learning and knowledge processing to which Morgan refers. Think about what science is showing about the role of brain neurons and neuro-chemicals in information flows, the growing understanding of the interdependency between brain regions and the brain's capacity to rewire and reform neural pathways (Stiles and Jernigan, 2010; Greenfield, 2008, Martin Gilles, 2017).

Social work and organisations: a brain?

If we think about organisations where social work operates as brains, following Morgan, we might think about learning and information processing within the organisation. Learning and reflective practice are basic to social work practice as we have mentioned in previous chapters, so we might think of how these processes work within our organisations. What supports them and encourages 'learning' and what happens with this new knowledge? How are the people we work with involved in these learning processes? What communication means are dominant? Think about the digital information flows in your social work organisation and where there are opportunities for face-to-face encounters?

Thinking with this metaphor of a 'brain' directs us into thinking about digital technological changes, the social processes outside the organisation that have enabled them and those that occur because of them. With digital technology and the use of emails, internet, and social media, contemporary organisations are immersed in information processing and this information can come at a pace. Think about how many emails you receive a day. How is this changing the nature of how we connect, communicate and relate with colleagues, organisational leaders and – of paramount importance – with the people we work with as social workers?

You may extend this thought process to consider the implications of digital technology in organisations where social workers work. Where is information stored? What are the implications for privacy and empowerment in the use of information about the people you work with as a social worker? What are the prevailing dynamics of human interaction and relationship-based practice through digital mediums? If identity is formed in the intersubjective space between you and another, what occurs in intersubjective cyberspace? How do we develop and maintain empathy as social workers? What of generational differences and access to digital technology? A brain metaphor also opens up images of surveillance, 'a super and all-knowing brain' (Morgan, 2006). This certainly has applicability in social work practice and for 'clients', or service users, with use of digitally stored and shared records and conditionality attached to the receipt of benefits and services.

It also is felt in workforces in how workers are treated and surveyed. The eighteenth-century writer Jeremy Bentham's panopticon, an inspection house to keep prisoners and others under surveillance, was used by Michael Foucault to theorise about the nature of power relations in institutions, workplaces and societies. Bentham, in his eighteenth-century pamphlet, calls the panoptican a means of 'obtaining power of mind over mind' (1995, p. 2). Foucault (1995, p. 217), using this metaphor, writes that we 'are neither in the amphitheatre, nor on the stage, but in the panoptic machine, invested by its effects of power which we bring to ourselves since we are part of its mechanism'. Not only are we watched over, but we introject these beliefs to the end where we survey ourselves. He explains further:

> In order to be exercised, this power had to be given the instrument of permanent, exhaustive, omnipresent surveillance, capable of making all visible, as long as it could itself remain invisible. It had to be like a faceless gaze that transformed the whole social body into a field of perception: thousands of eyes posted everywhere, mobile attentions ever on the alert.
>
> (Foucault, 1995, p. 464)

We have posed many questions in this section which have been triggered by thinking about social work in organisations using the metaphor of a brain, and this can take us down a particular pathway. Let's leave the brain image and move to the final metaphor we discuss in this chapter, namely the organisation as 'instrument of domination'.

Exercise – Imagining organisations which employ social workers

➤ Think about your employing organisation, or where you are doing or did your placement, as a human brain. What do you imagine?

➤ How does your organisation support learning processes?

➤ What are the implications of digital technology in organisations where social workers work?

➤ Where are the limits of thinking about social work organisations using a brain image?

Morgan's metaphor: organisation as 'instrument of domination'

The fourth and final metaphor we will describe is what Morgan defines as organisations as an 'instrument of domination' (2006). Morgan describes this as the 'ugly face' of organisations, reflecting on the role they play in exploitation and oppression. He writes, 'Throughout history, organization has been associated with processes of social domination where individuals or groups find ways of imposing their will on others' (Morgan, 2006, p. 293). With superb historical detail, Morgan (2006, pp. 293–329) canvasses what thinking with this metaphor in mind might bring to the surface: exploitation of the people who work in organisations (i.e., through working conditions and wage levels, actions of multi-nationals and conditions in supply chains); exploitation of people who use services or products (i.e., what they are charged); and exploitation of the natural environment in the course of making profits (i.e., pollution).

Morgan (2006) explores these themes through reference to the theoretical works of Karl Marx and Max Weber, and others, who wrote about oppression and reinforcement of dominant interests through organisations in capitalist social systems. For example, Morgan (2006, p. 331) writes, 'Many organizations are literally divided societies that perpetuate class warfare in the workplace'. These sociological ideas bring right to the fore issues of ideology and power. We read and see each and every day the 'ugly face' Morgan describes, and again, this raises the point that organisations are not neutral but the deliberate structuring of interests and power relations.

Social work and organisations: as 'instruments of domination'?

What would social workers see if we focus on this image of organisations reinforcing dominant power relations? Central to our social work imagination is addressing social injustices that are perpetuated in and by organisations. We seek to respond to these oppressive power relations. Market capitalism and profit maximisation agendas have impacted deeply on individual and collective livelihoods, wellbeing and hope for many as we discussed in Chapter 2. Economic inequality in countries such as the United Kingdom is growing in an alarmingly way. This is the context of social work practice with effects on the people, families and communities with whom we work.

The organisations that employ social workers can also be instruments of domination – and social workers who work in them can be agents of these practices by virtue of their work in these organisations. This is powerfully brought home in the 2016 Ken Loach film *I, Daniel Blake*, which tells the story of the protagonist Daniel and his dehumanising experiences of engaging with social welfare bureaucracy. Ferguson and Lavalette (2004) give us another way to think about this dimension of domination in the context of setting out an 'emancipatory social work practice'. In a powerful discussion on the applicability of Marx's notion of 'alienation' to social work they give examples of how the organisational setting of social work can alienate the people who use services and social workers; they can be alienated from a sense of agency and power, which is a necessary aspect of fulfilling social work's advocacy and social justice agenda, and from a sense of 'common humanity' (2004, p. 302).

We have given examples of the impacts of neo-liberal ideas and practices in previous chapters. Organisations that employ social workers are part of these broader human service delivery systems, which are located in an external environment influenced by political and ideological trends. In the United Kingdom, prevailing ideas are revealed by the use of language: vocabulary such as 'customer', 'business' planning, 'commissioner', 'co-production' and with it particular dynamics of power relations. Furthermore, oppressive practices can be so ingrained in organisational practices, decisions and behaviours that they may not be openly seen, talked about or challenged. It can just be 'the ways things are done', and be taken for granted.

The strength of our abilities to work for social justice are helped along if we are consciously aware of these organisational dilemmas and can situate these in a sociological context. But we do not want to think only in one way, and the quest is to also think of how this metaphor does not fit the organisation we know and work within. How is the organisation delivering social work also a tool for liberation and empowerment? How does the organisation use its learning processes to respond to internal oppressive practices?

Exercise – Imagining organisations which employ social workers as an instrument of domination

Think about the image of an organisation as an instrument of domination. What thoughts come to your mind?

Think about this image in relation to where you are doing your placement or work as a social worker.

Where are the limits of thinking about organisations this way?

Conclusions

Just as Albus Dumbledore in the Harry Potter series used a pensieve bowl to sort his thoughts, we need a way to sort out our experiences and thoughts about organisations as an ongoing project. Morgan (2006) assembled a process for using metaphors to 'read' organisational life from sociological and organisational theory. In this chapter we have been selective in using four of Morgan's metaphors to illustrate the value of such an approach and also to explore dimensions of organisations of relevance to social work. From our brief application of four of Morgan's metaphors to organisations where social workers practice, we have stood and looked from four places. What does the composite picture look like?

The extensive 'machine' thinking and practices in social work organisational settings is made visible (i.e., neo-liberal practices in 'top-down' funding and regulatory specifications, outcomes and performance indicators, prescribed work practices, risk aversion, technical bureaucratic practices). Thinking this way also crystallises the clash of a machine-like approach with social work's human and heart-filled process. Switching perspectives to view organisations where social workers are located as an 'organism' animates images of interdependency (i.e. holism in human experience; interdependency at a system level), the diversity of the organisational settings of social work, ecological thinking and the importance of organisational openness in a responsive and critical social work.

The brain metaphor drew us to the construction of learning and development processes within social work organisations and the question of how contextually relevant learning is enabled in ways where the knowledge generated can contribute to richer social work practice. The expansion of digital technology in organisations, with both its empowering and disempowering aspects, raises important questions about the relation between social work values and the use of information. Finally, imagining an organisation with an 'ugly face' brings home a fundamental purpose of social work, which is a practice to challenge and address oppressive social relations. This includes attention to what is occurring in the organisational setting of our own practice.

Practising social work sociologically

> ➤ The social justice challenges of the times manifest in organisational practices. This behoves social workers to have tools to think deeply about working in organisations and how organisations work, if social justice goals are to be realised.

> ➤ In using Morgan's organisational metaphors, we are illustrating a way to prise open other ways to see and think about what we might 'take for granted' in working in organisations where social work practice is located.

> ➤ This metaphorical approach is a means to engage in an imaginative process which Morgan describes as a way to 'tap' into memories, experiences and intuitive knowledge.

> ➤ An active sociological social work practice is strengthened by attention to the organisational context of social work and organisational change.

9

Using Research in Practice

What is research?

Research always aims to increase knowledge in a particular area in response to a question or focus of investigation. Social research is specifically concerned with social worlds and humans and can include all matter of topics, social issues, human experiences, social movements and societal phenomena. Although the concept of social research may seem somewhat broad, it shares something that is common to all types of research: that is, social research represents a very specific and narrowed-down area of systematic investigation or inquiry. In this chapter, we argue that a sociological social work practice in research helps to frame what we explore and how we do this in a critical and contextual way. Yet we need to extend our critical lens to better understand who has had the dominant voice in research, and why. Gayle Letherby succinctly articulates this when she states: 'Sociology, my own academic discipline, clearly demonstrates male bias' (Letherby, 2003, p. 20).

The importance of social research to social work scholarship and practice cannot be underestimated. The things that have historically been at the centre of mainstream research have been defined and investigated by people who have had access to power: and these have been white, middle-class men. Jane Addams and Alice Salomon as researchers showed another way. What we see in contemporary research is the appreciation of the 'overlooked norm'; the everyday and mundane routines which shape human existence are increasingly being empirically explored. Through research, we can identify trends, experiences and patterns in experience. As Gagnon and Simon point out:

> Underlying all human activity, regardless of the field or its stage of development, there exist metaphors or informing imageries – commonly unnamed until they lose their potency – that shape thought, experiment, and the directions of research.

This chapter therefore examines social research in relation to our socio-logical social work perspective. There has been an increased interest in the application of empirical knowledge to social work practice contexts which is evident in the rise of so-called evidence-based practice (also referred to as 'research-based practice'), which we critically explore. As we know as social scientists, in our frame of reference research is always linked to not only ethics and values but also to our epistemological orientation. Evidence therefore becomes contextual and subjective. This chapter begins, therefore, by asking the question: how do we know what we know?

Objective knowledge?

How do we know that a particular practice approach 'works' in the way that it is intended? What of the views of the people who are at the centre of our social work practice? What is the role of the professional in speak-ing on behalf of human experience? We see that the rise of the profes-sional and the use of research to 'prove' a particular practice approach's efficacy are both symptoms of some of the shifts we have explored in this book. For example, the increasing rationalisation in public sector organisations has seen an unprecedented need for social workers to justify budgets and 'prove' that their services are cost-effective. Here, a 'scientific method' is one that dominates and brings prestige and can be used to justify expenditure on particular programmes or services. Reid points out that research is used in direct service as well as being used to better under-stand how people engage in problem-solving and navigating inequalities:

> Historically, the influence of science on direct social work practice has taken two forms. One is the use of the scientific method to shape practice activi-ties, for example, gathering evidence and forming hypotheses about a client's problem. The other form is the provision of scientific knowledge about human beings, their problems and ways of resolving them.
>
> (Reid, 1998, p. 3).

One need only to turn on the radio or television or other media to hear or watch an expert give advice and insight into particular issues. Often these experts are active researchers – professionals who have worked in some capacity with people and have additional knowledge through empirical investigation into a particular issue. When we come across knowledge in this way we may be prompted to think about our own experiences of the particular phenomenon under discussion. We can then find ourselves agreeing or disagreeing with the expert's assessment of this issue. Take, for example, the issue of depression.

Experts will range in their approach to depression and will depend on whether they come from, say, psychology or psychiatry to social work or sociology. The differences in the worldviews between these disciplines can be enormous. The way that depression is defined by medical sciences may be at odds with sociological understandings of the category of 'mental health', for example. This means that not only is depression viewed differently between disciplines and professions, but that the very underlying worldview that underpins the disciplinary boundaries will differ. The worldview or epistemology gets to the heart of the way in which a profession or an individual will see the world around them.

If we continue with the example of depression, for example, a psychiatrist might be interested in the individual's history and biography. They might be particularly interested in the way in which biological and social factors intersect and will assess the individual's situation and make a determination as to the cause of the presenting depression. Treatment options might include therapy but may also include the prescription of pharmaceuticals to address problems in brain chemistry. This approach might therefore lead researchers to be curious about particular issues related to, for example, pharmaceuticals as a response to depression. The way that research questions are framed is influenced by the underlying 'worldview' of the discipline or profession. Recent psychiatric research in Denmark, for example, sought to understand the impact of the use of combined medications and their efficacy in treating depression (Köhler et al., 2016). What are some of the other ways this issue of depression might be approached?

Social workers, more so than other professions, are committed to understanding individual experiences and noting patterns in the social world. So too are sociological perspectives interested in the connection between individual experience and social conditions. For example, a social scientist interested in researching depression might therefore be curious about the role of social inequality and its connection to mental health (Muntaner et al., 2013). It is therefore important that social workers understand the underlying worldview or 'paradigm' which informs knowledge about depression (Huang and Fang, 2015) but also the ways in which one's worldview influences the choice of research and the conceptualisation of the research problem (Crotty, 2007). One way to think about this is to reflect on what we think is 'true'. What can we confidently state about the social world which will apply to everyone? Let's look further now at how and when we can make knowledge claims, or whether in fact we can state that something is 'true' for everyone (Figure 9.1).

Figure 9.1 The stick

Take a look at Figure 9.1. What do you see? What one word would you use to describe the image? Do you think that one word can capture meaning for everyone in the world? Let's assume that you use the word 'stick' to define what you see in the image. Do you think that everyone would see the image in the same way as you? That is, can we assert this meaning across all aspects of identity? Let's assume, for example, that we gave the object to a child, aged around five or six years old. What word might they use for the object? Would their conceptualisation of the object be similar or identical to your own? Take a look at Figure 9.2.

Figure 9.2   Stick swords

The way a child might conceptualise the object will invariably depend upon how they use the object. In the image above we can see two children using the sticks as swords. Does this change the meaning? What if you asked the children to name the object – would they say 'sword'? What does this mean for the overall meaning of the object? Does this mean that the object can no longer be universally referred to as a 'stick'? What if a child used the object as a 'wand'? Does this still make the object a 'stick'? Whose meanings are paramount? Whose voice ought to be able to define meaning? Is there a hierarchy of meaning and who has the power to decide? What if we spoke to the child about the object and explored their meanings alongside those of an adult? Can you imagine what kinds of conversation might take place? Should the adult's meanings override the child's? Already we can see that there are difficulties with assuming that one's perspective applies for everyone. If you were to give the object to someone who works with wood to make objects, they might see it as a resource or a piece of art. A landscaper or gardener might see the stick as potential bark chips. Again, the meaning changes in these different contexts.

Social science researchers generally take a complex view of social reality in that they recognise that particular variables such as one's age, occupation, culture and so on will influence both the way they view the social world as well as the meanings they attach to objects, relationships and interactions. This is connected to the theoretical and epistemological underpinnings of the social sciences. Thus, this kind of truth-seeking in research becomes more problematic than first expected. Whereas researchers from the pure sciences – say, biology or medicine – will generally take the view that a 'fact' is a 'fact' for everyone, social science researchers will often take a contradictory view in which the social world is constructed by its agents. This underlying worldview is often referred to as epistemology. Epistemology is important to consider in the context of research design because it influences the choices researchers make in relation to the methods used as well as the research question itself (Crotty, 2007).

The research question

Social work researchers are interested in research for a number of reasons, and the questions we seek to answer and explore will be many and varied. These may relate to understanding the effectiveness of a particular intervention as noted earlier, or research may be designed to advance theory, influence policy, or understand more about the causes of social issues in order to address them better. As with the researcher's underlying epistemological perspective, the research question will be guided by the purpose of the research itself. Important questions need to be addressed when constructing the research question such as: Why is the research important? What will the research help me and others to better understand? To whom is the research aimed? How will community participation or involvement take place in the research? Some researchers refer to this as the 'so what?' question. It can be helpful to imagine one needs to answer the question: why is this research important? If research is to be undertaken it cannot be without purpose.

Sociological social workers have a critical lens (Dunk-West and Verity, 2013). Often social workers engage in critical thinking without naming it and it is sometimes the case that social work students become confused between critical thinking and providing a 'critique'. Although these terms are interrelated, the manifestation of critical thinking is important to the construction of the research problem, and the research question itself. A helpful activity in engaging in critical thinking for day-to-day objects can help social workers re-frame or re-orient the research question. One suggested activity promotes thinking of an object and relating it back to its historical and social contexts, understanding which groups benefit and suffer from the object and re-imagining the object with the removal of power inequalities (Kaufman, 1997). At the heart of social work is the commitment to social justice which promotes an awareness of power in practice as well as social activism to remove inequality (Gair, 2016). Thus, engaging in exercises which promote the re-conceptualisation of a research problem alongside a critical lens is vital. We argue that researchers engaging in critical thinking when constructing research questions are less likely to reproduce inequality and unequal power relationships.

Critical thinking in the research question design stage equates to the application of the sociological imagination so that the researcher positions themselves in their social and historical contexts. Sociology established itself as a discipline through the replication of the pure sciences: historically a time in which '... the only sociology was [seen as] mediocre and empirical, without any theoretical or indeed empirical inspiration behind it' (Bourdieu, 1991, p. 5). This view shifted in the 1960s and beyond, a period marked by the engagement of newer ways of researching and theorising about social life, and Bourdieu notes that empirical work as well as theory-building occur in broader contexts:

> To say that there are social conditions for the production of truth is to say that there is a politics of truth, an action constantly exercised in order to defend and improve the functioning of the social universes in which rational principles are applied and truth comes into being
>
> (Bourdieu, 1990, p. 32).

For researchers in organisations, the values of the organisation also influence the design of research and the conceptualisation of the research problem, and how the research will be done. Being aware of these influences and engaging in a critical analysis of why the research is important is central to sociological social work practice in research. We will now explore some of the methodologies and methods used by social researchers.

Social research methodology and methods

Quantitative statistics help to better understand social trends, behaviours and inequalities that are of interest to social researchers. One example of this kind of research is the tracking of gender inequality in the workforce. Recent studies point to the sustained inequality in relation to pay for men and women in the workforce, with women consistently earning less than their male counterparts (Angelov et al., 2016). Large datasets help to reveal what is happening in broader social contexts and this kind of research can assist in looking beyond national borders. Crime statistics similarly connect individual issues with social problems, for example sexual assaults primarily occur by male perpetrators towards women (Campbell, Wasco et al., 2005; Victorian Centres Against Sexual Assault, 2017). Such statistics can assist researchers in delving further into social conditions. Both examples – gendered inequality in the workforce in relation to pay and sexual violence towards women – can help to question the ways in which individuals are raised in particular social conditions and subsequently question how gender plays a part in social inequality.

Social scientists are interested not only in the representation of broader statistics, but can analyse how variables such as gender, education and other identity markers shape outcomes for individuals. Here patterns are important and researchers can see whether particular variables influence social problems, for example. Whereas statistical representations help to frame broader social conditions and are applicable to a particular population, they cannot reveal the particular individual experiences. To use the example of gendered inequality relating to the pay gap, we know that women are more likely to experience lower rates of pay across the life course but statistics cannot tell us *how individual women experience inequality*.

Qualitative research helps to connect the social issues revealed through quantitative data analysis to individual experiences of particular phenomena. Here, the sociological imagination is important to social researchers because it assists with asking more specific questions that can connect societal conditions to individual stories. Social research methodologies such as phenomenology offer social researchers the opportunity to understand social phenomena as it is subjectively experienced by individuals. Despite the focus on subjective experience, data analysis looks for patterns in individual narratives and connects these together, thus bringing about new insights into social issues.

For example, if we return to the example at the beginning of the chapter where we explored the meaning connected to an object, we reflected on the ways in which adults and children interpret objects differently. In research, we might be interested in better understanding the role and meaning of other concepts, such as 'favourite possessions', for example, for both adults and children. This kind of research approach asserts that individual or subjective knowledge requires further analysis and subjective accounts would help to find patterns in particular types of experiences. Once the patterns have been identified through data analysis, the role of the social researcher is to generate a broader finding to explain the overall finding of the research. Here, social researchers will often use a 'grounded theory' approach where the research findings point to an existing or new theory to explain social phenomena. One example of this kind of research sought to better understand the role that possessions had for individuals. The finding of the research was that there were particular meanings attached to particular objects. The researcher therefore theorised that particular possessions are a kind of externalised sense of self, and argued that possessions represent the 'extended self' (Belk, 1988).

The focus on individual experiences and the concept that meaning-making is subjective is one which resonates with social work theory and practice. Asking questions such as 'what was this like for you?' can apply not only in social work practice with individuals but also for social workers undertaking research. Here, a social work practice approach, informed by social work theory, is easily transferrable across contexts.

Methods

Social workers in practice with individuals, groups and communities possess many skills which are easily translated into research. Micro research approaches, such as those which focus on day-to-day meanings, gestures and symbols, have an established theoretical and historical affinity with social work (Forte, 2004). For example, interviews require similar social work skills such as empathy and tuning in (Wilson and Kelly, 2010), establishing rapport and asking open ended-questions to better understand a particular issue from the perspective of the person being interviewed. Similarly, social workers who work in communities will often undertake community assessments – forums and focus groups can be used to generate data to better understand community needs and draw from the same skill set. Social workers often work 'in situ' meaning that they are enmeshed within the community, physically visiting people's homes and assisting in the provision of particular services to an area. This kind of work is transferrable to ethnographic research. One example of this type of research in social work scholarship is Harry Ferguson's ethnographic work with child protection social workers (Ferguson, 2011). Organisational ethnography can generate insights into organisational structures, processes and systems (White et al., 2010).

Micro sociological approaches are often useful in social work research because of the emphasis on the lived experience of people and the assumption that people make sense of the world around them in varying ways that are specific to themselves and dependent upon one's biography, worldviews, values and sense of themselves. The researcher in this approach is seen as partnering with the participant in the context of the social world. Schutz says:

> ... in terms of common-sense thinking in everyday life men [and women] have knowledge of these various dimensions of the social world in which they live ... common-sense knowledge of everyday life is sufficient for coming to terms

with fellow-men [and fellow-women], cultural objects, social institutions – in brief, with social reality ... because the world (the natural and the social one) is from the outset an intersubjective world and because ... our knowledge of it is in various ways socialized.

(Schutz, 1954, p. 492)

For symbolic interactionists, the small ways in which we communicate with one another is laden with meaning. For the researcher using this approach, it is vital that the meaning of the participant's narrative is clear and able to be gleaned through the use of an appropriate research method. Here, the researcher is required to delve into the sense-making and meanings that participants hold for their interactions and communications. The researcher uses their sense of curiosity and imagination in trying to understand the participant's reality. For data to be able to reflect this understanding, there needs to be an active desire on the part of the researcher to search for these meanings:

... data are valid when a deep mutual understanding has been achieved between interviewer and respondent. The practical consequence is that most interactionists reject prescheduled standardized interviews in favour of open-ended interviews. The latter allow respondents to use their own particular way of defining the world [and] assume that no fixed sequence of questions is suitable to all respondents.

(Fielding, 1996, p. 151)

New kinds of research in new times

As we have discussed in other chapters of this book, we now live in an age of unprecedented technologically advanced communication. In an age where internet access ensures connectivity for a range of people, researchers have access to a new kind of 'informal data'. Let's imagine that we wanted to better understand the challenges for people who are new to parenting. A researcher could access online forums where people discuss their experiences and make some conclusions about the prevalent issues for people who use internet forums to share parenting challenges. Is it ethical to involve research subjects who do not know they are research subjects? One argument is that in contributing to online discussions such as forums and blogs, people inadvertently provide 'permission' for others to access their information given that they are aware that the internet is a public space. By contrast, there are a range of ethical conventions in research which establish the notion of 'informed consent', which is vital to consider in social work research, particularly for minority groups, which historically have been researched 'on' rather than researched 'with' (McInroy, 2016). One thing is for certain: in our contemporary landscape, we have more than enough data to better understand humans and their movements within their environments. In the next section of this chapter we will consider 'big data' alongside the ethical issues raised in relation to research.

Big data

The term 'big data' relates not only to the amount and range of data which is collected by businesses, governments and a range of organisations, it also relates to the speed at which data is generated in contemporary times, aided by the rapid rate of technological advance (Connelly et al., 2016). These changes have also opened up an unprecedented desire for an opportunity to track individuals' movements or engage in 'data tracking', resulting in a 'datafication of everything' (Millington and Millington, 2015). For example, computer software and internet connectivity has resulted in a kind of idiosyncratic marketing where items for purchase are targeted based upon the individual through the tracking of one's interests gleaned from internet browsing history and behaviours. Yet can these kinds of data help in making sense of the social world? There is some contention about the utility of data derived from the unassuming internet user and ethical considerations ought to be combined to justify whether research around big data is possible. However, it can be said that the future of research in the social sciences will have to grapple with the meanings, ethics and usefulness that the age of big data brings.

Conclusions

This chapter has considered the broader social contexts in which social work research takes place. From who gets to ask the questions to the underlying epistemological perspective – we argue that it is crucial for the social work researcher to engage in a deeper level of understanding than simply applying the status quo to investigating research problems. In this chapter, we have argued that social and political contexts as well as technological change are future challenges to social work research. Since research is increasingly becoming a part of the rationalised world of social work provision, critically evaluating the broader social conditions in which research takes place is crucial to this endeavour.

Practising social work sociologically

Practising social work sociologically as a researcher involves understanding historically who has had the dominant voice to define, research and theorise about social life. In this chapter, we have also explored the role that research can play in contemporary research and we have explored some of the ethical challenges of research in our shifting times. Practising social work sociologically involves employing a critical lens to knowledge claims and understanding particular research methodologies and practice wisdom alongside the broader pressures that organisational settings can bring about. Specifically, practising social work sociologically in relation to research involves the following:

➤ Understanding power in relation to the asking, reporting and recording of research problems and addressing this power imbalance

➤ Identifying the broader social, political and cultural conditions in which research takes place

➤ Anticipating the future directions for research and the ethical challenges that will be faced

➤ Applying a social work ethics lens to navigating inequality and ethical conflicts in research.

10

Conclusions and Future Directions

Introduction

In this concluding chapter, we re-visit the key ideas presented in this book and look to the future to envisage how sociological social work might help in navigating challenges. Sociological social work, we argue, is vital for practice in an increasingly complex world in which inequalities and injustice endure and in a world which is rapidly changing in the face of technological developments and emerging dynamics of globalisation. It is also a world full of hopes and inventiveness, and where there are numerous examples of social solidarity, spirits of reform and justice that also shape our collective social imaginary.

Throughout this book, we encourage a critical perspective in which our national and international perspectives are compared and examined in the light of social, economic and political shifts. We have highlighted the need to think differently about taken-for-granted assumptions and to employ sociological perspectives in order to enrich our practice. John Berger articulates why it is crucial to 'see' what we 'look at'. He says:

> We only see what we look at. To look is an act of choice. As a result of this act, what we see is brought within our reach – though not necessarily within arm's reach. To touch something is to situate oneself in relation to it. ... We never look at just one thing; we are always looking at the relation between things and ourselves. Our vision is continually active, continually moving, continually holding things in a circle around itself, constituting what is present to us as we are.
>
> John Berger, Ways of Seeing

The approach in this book draws from social work's rich history with sociology. We have extended such an approach to fit the shifting landscape within which we are immersed. Whereas psychological approaches locate the individual as the focus, we argue that sociological social work entails a broader approach in which historically located social, political, economic and cultural conditions combine to create one's lived experience. We have followed the well-trodden path that places central social work's historical commitment to psycho-social work. This necessitates a dual focus on both the individual as situated in the social and historical conditions that constitute and shape human experience. These are simultaneously local, national and global. Yet sociological social work is more than simple acknowledgement of the context of the work, albeit that is important.

In this book we have drawn from social work history and sociological scholarship and presented this kind of theory as a way to orient practice, identify taken-for-granted meanings and provide rich interpretations and in-depth analyses. We have also demonstrated a range of theoretical approaches from sociology and engaged with the tensions and conflicts between opposing theoretical traditions. We do this so that social work students and practitioners can adapt approaches and see alternative framing of a particular social issue. It is this presentation of a range of approaches that engages the curious social worker: theory ought to be interpreted through a socio-political and ethical lens and we hope that this approach provides social workers with additional 'tools' to enhance their practice.

Tools for practising social work sociologically

Throughout the book, we have drawn together key ways for practising social work sociologically, and these have been drawn from many ideas from social work and sociology. Indeed, the very act of critically engaging with ideas is a doorway into the approach we present; we are collective thinkers and draw on bodies of knowledge and insights from experience, including tacit knowledge. A common theme across this book is that we are reflexive actors and social pattern makers, identifying and recognising the historical and current socio-cultural and political events which influence contemporary social work practice, and from this basis engaging with the people with whom we work. We seek to know about how this impacts on their day-to-day lives. Yet the very ways in which we think require re-orienting. Sociological perspectives assist us in better understanding the dimensions of social issues and it is through scholarship that social work practice is sharpened, heightened and enriched. This thinking and inquiry process does not stand still and our understandings are made and remade.

Mills' craft of using a 'sociological imagination' give us an order or structure for imaginative habits in social work practice, which include holding an ongoing capacity to be curious, to make comparisons and connections between events, thoughts, ideas and experience, and, in these processes, to surround yourself with sources of support and encouragement. The tools combine thinking and creativity tools, as well as tools about 'being' as a social worker. These include practical ideas to maintain an international perspective about our common humanity; engagement in critical and imaginative thinking as a purposeful habit; recognising the dynamic social dimensions to relationships; the power relations and contextual factors that impact on the organisations in which social work takes place; the relations between self, agency and structure; and the temporal plane, which is important given that we live in another time in human history where time and space have been reconceptualised. Each has in common that they give us a way to see and re-see, in a continuous process of coming to better understand the social worlds in which people live, and in which we practise our social work.

These domains and tools of practising social work sociologically are summarised in the following box.

	PRACTISING SOCIAL WORK SOCIOLOGICALLY
Learning from history	A focus on social work and sociology is part of social work heritage. We learn from history the following: • The importance in social work of empathy and identification of our common humanity • International sensibilities are needed in a global world • Creative enquiry and learning is part of understanding underlying structural patterns, or what we might take for granted, and using this to inform what might be done • Never to keep critical deep thinking and action apart • Action is needed that contributes to change at a societal level and change at the community, family and individual level

Imagination in social work	Creativity and imagination are essential elements of a sociologically informed social work:
	
	• Social workers are agents in imaginative processes at two levels: to see and create a possible, and see the links between the micro (individual social system) and macro (societal dimensions)
	• Mills' art of a 'sociological imagination' (1970) give us a structure for imaginative habits in social work practice:
	
	   ○ Be curious
	   ○ Draw comparisons and make connections
	   ○ Surround yourself with sources of support and encouragement

Social relationships and capital	Working with individuals, groups and communities, sociological social work involves: • Appreciation that humans are in social environments and are social actors • Communities offer actors opportunities to come together and generate social change. Here the social worker's role is as a facilitator for positive, community-led social change • Understanding the patterned and shared meanings and practices and looking for exceptions, innovations and resilience. • Focusing at multi-levels through interventions
Time and space	Understanding the role of time and space involves practising social work sociologically by: • Identifying and recognising the historical events which influence contemporary social work practice and being able to engage with the people with whom we work about how this impacts on their day-to-day lives • Appreciating and naming the new and innovative ways that time and space have been reconceptualised in contemporary social work practice and utilising new kinds of 'rich practice' • Looking to nations to better understand how legal, ethical and social conditions understand, name and address social inequalities
Social work in organisations	Practising social work sociologically in relation to organisations requires: • A conceptual framework in which to think about organisations as social systems and social relationships • Thinking reflexively about the organisational context of social work and continuity and change, to see and understand the internal features of an organisation and the impact of the external environment • Using organisational metaphors (i.e., Morgan's images of organisations as 'organisms', 'machines', 'brains' and so) in an imaginative process is a means to tap into experience, feelings and intuitive knowledge about organisations in an active sociological social work practice
Agency and self	Practising social work sociologically in relation to self, agency and structure involves the following: • Understanding theories of identity which draw upon scholarship in relation to social and historical contexts • Reflexivity that is part of a broader cultural shift towards individual experience • Empowerment that is problematic if it does not take into account social structure • Social work that must be oriented towards social structure and use approaches which respond to both individual and social issues

Social work research	Practising social work sociologically as a researcher involves:
	• Understanding power in relation to the asking, reporting and recording of research problems and addressing this power imbalance
	• Identifying the broader social, political and cultural conditions in which research takes place
	• Anticipating the future directions for research and the ethical challenges that will be faced
	• Applying a social work ethics lens to navigating inequality and ethical conflicts in research

Table 10.1 Domains and Tools for Practising Social Work Sociologically

Future directions

We started this book with asking the reader to examine planet Earth from the International Space Station (ISS). As we have explored throughout this book, there are a rich and complex range of issues present in the contemporary world, some of which we have discussed in more depth than others. These include:

➤ The changing nature of 'work' and employment as global economic systems change;

➤ Technological developments with implications for individual and social life;

➤ Environmental change;

➤ Insecurity in relation to fuel, weather and climate systems;

➤ Political and social developments which are reinforcing and challenging conventional practices and power relations;

➤ Actions across the world where people, groups and communities are working for peace and justice;

➤ Persisting inequalities in relation to health, poverty, and access to education and actions to close these gaps;

➤ Increasing narratives and counter-narratives of risk;

➤ Market-led ideology and subsequent social work service provision.

In this book we have offered tools to understand and meet these challenges and opportunities, and enable social workers to continue to best support those with whom they work. This includes challenging systems and institutions that are oppressive. We have argued that imagination, engagement and critical thinking are central to the process of distinguishing between the individual and the social as well as understanding how individuals and the social are influenced, shaped and made and re-made. Given that social workers in the contemporary world understand too well that sometimes it is the very systems in which they work that re-enforce social divisions and contribute to injustice, this is no easy task. Instead, we suggest that social work must continue to remain focused on its mission to facilitate positive change and work to promote social justice principles and practices. Sociological theory helps us to navigate this tricky terrain. It reminds us that we are situated in history, assists us to name and identify the taken-for-granted assumptions and meanings imbedded in the systems within which we work. Bringing together sociological theory is both an art and a social science, and one that is embedded in the rich history of social work as a discipline.

References

Addams, J. (ud) '20 years at the Hull-House', in *Jane Addams: The Collected Works*, Kindle E-Books.

Addams, J. (ud) *Jane Addams: The Collected Works*, Kindle E-Books.

Addams, J. (1902) 'The -No. 13' (March 29), pp. 284–286.

Angell, J. (1906) 'Imagination', Chapter 8 in *Psychology: An Introductory Study of the Structure and Function of Human Conscious*, Third Edition, revised. Henry Holt and Company, New York, pp. 161–183. Accessed from the Mead Project source page.

Appadurai, A. (1996) *Modernity at Large: Cultural Dimensions of Globalization*, University of Minnesota, Minnesota.

Bauman, Z. (1998) *Globalization – The Human Consequences,* Polity Press in association with Blackwell Publishers, Cambridge.

Bauman, Z. (2001) *Community: Seeking Safety in an Insecure World*, Polity Press, Cambridge.

Bauman, Z and May, T. (2001) *Thinking Sociologically*, Blackwell Publishing, Oxford.

Bentham, J. (1995) The Panopticon Writings. Ed. Miran Bozovic, London: Verso. http://www.ics.uci.edu/~djp3/classes/2012_01_INF241/papers/PANOPTICON.pdf. Accessed 19th September 2017.

Berger, J. (1977). *Ways of Seeing*. London, Penguin Books.

Bogo, M. and Vayda, E. (1987) *The Practice of Field Instruction in Social Work*, University of Toronto Press, Toronto.

Bolton, G. (2001) *Reflective Practice*, Paul Chapman Publishing Limited, Sage Publications, London.

Bourdieu, P. (1986) 'The forms of capital', in J. Richardson (Ed.), *Handbook of Theory and Research for the Sociology of Education*, Greenwood, Westport, pp. 241–258.

Bourdieu, P. (1991) *Language and Symbolic Power,* Harvard University Press, Cambridge.

Bourdieu, P. and Wacquant, L. (1992) *An Invitation to Reflexive Sociology,* University of Chicago Press, Chicago.

Brewer, J. (2004) 'Imagining *The Sociological Imagination*: The biographical context of a sociological classic', *British Journal of Sociology*, Vol. 55, pp. 317–333.

Bryson, L. and Mowbray, M. (1981), 'Community': The Spray-on Solution. *Australian Journal of Social Issues*, 16: 255–267. doi:10.1002/j.1839-4655.1981.tb00713.x

Bryson, L. and Verity, F. (2009) 'Australia: From wage earners to neo-liberal welfare state', in G. Craig, and P. Alcock (Eds.), *International Social Policy: Welfare Regimes in the Developed World*, Second Edition, Palgrave, New York, pp. 66–87.

Castells, M. (1996) *The Rise of the Network Society*, Blackwell Publishers, Boston.

Cockburn, C. (2015) 'Transversal politics: A practice of peace', February 2015 Pacifist Feminism .

Cohen, A. (2013) The Cohen Interviews: Clare Winnicott (nee BRITTON) – Interview no 24, Edited by Tim Cook and Harry Marsh. Available at: http://www2.warwick.ac.uk/services/library/mrc/explorefurther/speakingarchives/socialwork/929.publ_no_24_winnicott.pdf. Accessed 26th September 2017.

Comartin, E. and Gonzalez-Prendes, A. (2011) 'Dissonance between personal and professional values: Resolution of an ethical dilemma', *Journal of Social Work Values and Ethics*, Vol. 8, No. 2, pp. 1–14.

Compton, B. and Galaway, B. (1979) *Social Work Processes*, Dorsey Press, Homewood.

Cooperrider, D. and Whitney, D. (2005) *Appreciative Inquiry: A Positive Revolution in Change*, Berrett-Koehler Publishers, San Francisco.

Corlett, A. and Clarke, S. (2017) *Living Standards 2017: The Past, Present and Possible Future of UK Incomes*, Resolution Foundation, London.

Crimeen, K. and Wilson, L. (1997) 'Economic rationalism or social justice: A challenge for social workers', *Australian Social Work*, 50, (pp. 47–52).

Crotty, M. (2007). *The Foundations of Social Research: Meaning and Perspective in the Research Process* London, Sage.

Csikszentmihalyi, M. (1990) *Flow: The Psychology of Optimal Experience*, Harper Perennial Modern Classics, New York.

Cunningham, S. and Cunningham, J. (2008) *Sociology and Social Work*, Learning Matters Ltd, Exeter.

Czarniawska-Joerges, B. (1992) *Exploring Complex Organizations: A Cultural Perspective*, Sage Publications, Newbury Park.

D'Cruz, H. and Jones, M. (2004) *Social Work Research: Ethical and Political Contexts*, Sage Publications, London.

D'Cruz, H., Gillingham, P. and Melendez, S. (2007). Reflexivity, its meaning and relevance for social work: A critical review of the literature. *British Journal of Social Work*, 37, 73–90.

Davies, M. (1991) 'Sociology and social work: A misunderstood relationship', Chapter One in M. Davies (Ed.), *The Sociology of Social Work*, Routledge, London.

De Block, A. and Adriaens, P. R. (2013) 'Pathologizing sexual deviance: A history', *The Journal of Sex Research*, Vol. 50, pp. 276–298.

DEEP. (undated) *Magic Moments in Care Homes: Inspire, Motivate, Support*, Swansea University, Swansea.

Dickinson, E. (1999) *The Poems of Emily Dickinson* (Reading Edition R. W. Franklin), Harvard University Press, Cambridge.

Dominelli, L. (1997) *Sociology for Social Work*, Palgrave, Hampshire.

Dunk-West, P. (2011) 'Everyday sexuality and identity: De-differentiating the sexual self in social work', in P. Dunk-West and T. Hafford-Letchfield (Eds.), *Sexual Identities and Sexuality in Social Work: Research and Reflections from Women in the Field*, Ashgate, Farnham.

Dunk-West (2012). "The Sexual Self and Social Work and Policy, or, Why Teenage Pregnancy Prevention Programmes Miss the Point." *Social Work & Society* 10(2): 1–13.

Dunk-West, P. (2013b) 'Gender, agency and the sexual self: A theoretical model for social work', *Advances in Social Work and Welfare Education,* Vol. 15, pp. 31–46.

Dunk-West, P. (2013b) *How to be a Social Worker: A Critical Guide for Students,* Palgrave MacMillan, Basingstoke.

Dunk-West, P. and Verity, F. (2013) *Sociological Social Work,* Ashgate, Farnham.

Durkheim, E. (1984) *The Division of Labor in Society,* Free Press, New York.

Eldridge, J. and Crombie, A. (1974) *A Sociology of Organisations.* George Allen and Unwin Ltd., London.

Elliott, A. (2003) *Critical Visions: New Directions in Social Theory,* Rowman and Littlefield, Oxford.

Faubert, M. (2017) 'Granville Sharp's manuscript letter to the Admiralty on the Zong Massacre: A new discovery in the British Library', *Slavery and Abolition,* Vol. 38, No. 1, pp. 178–195.

Ferguson, H. (2001) 'Social work, individualization and life politics', *British Journal of Social Work,* Vol. 31, pp. 41–55.

Ferguson, H. (2008) 'Liquid social work: Welfare interventions as mobile practices', *British Journal of Social Work,* Vol. 38, pp. 561–579.

Ferguson, H. (2009) 'Driven to care: The car, automobility and social work', *Mobilities,* Vol. 4, pp. 275–293.

Ferguson, H. (2011) *Child Protection Practice,* Palgrave MacMillan, Basingstoke.

Ferguson, I. and Lavalette, M. (2004) 'Beyond power discourse: Alienation and social work', *British Journal of Social Work,* 34, pp. 297–312.

Ferguson, I. and Lavalette, M. (2013) 'Crisis, austerity and the future(s) of social work in the UK', *Critical and Radical Social Work,* vol 1, no 1, pp. 95–110.

Feustel, A. (ud) *The Significance of International Relations and Cooperation in the Works of Alice Salomon.* Original German version in: Ariadne. Forum für Frauen- und Geschlechtergeschichte, Vol. 49 (2006), pp. 24–29 (Translated by Swantje Siepmann).

Fook, J. (1999) 'Critical reflexivity in education and practice', in B. Pease and J. Fook (Eds.), *Transforming Social Work Practice: Postmodern Critical Perspectives,* Routledge, London.

Ford, M. (2015) *The Rise of Robots – Technology and the Threat of a Jobless Future,* Basic Books, New York.

Forte, J. A. (2004). "Symbolic Interactionism and Social Work: A Forgotten Legacy, Part 2." *Families in Society* 85(4): 521–530.

Foucault, M. (1995) *Discipline & Punish: The Birth of the Prison,* Vintage Books, New York, pp. 195–228 (translated from the French by Alan Sheridan 1977).

Froggett, L. (2002) *Love, Hate and Welfare, Psychosocial Approaches to Policy and Practice,* Policy Press, Bristol.

Furedi, F. (2004). *Therapy Culture: Cultivating Vulnerability in an Uncertain Age.* London, Routledge.

Gardiner, M. (2004) 'Everyday utopianism', *Cultural Studies,* Vol. 18, pp. 228–254.

Garrett, P. M. (2007) 'The relevance of Bourdieu for social work: A reflection on obstacles and omissions', *Journal of Social Work,* Vol. 7, No. 3, pp. 355–379.

Garrett, P. M. (2012). 'Re-enchanting social work? The emerging 'spirit' of social work in an age of economic crisis', *British Journal of Social Work*, Vol. 44, pp. 503–521.

Garrett, P. M. (2013) *Social Work and Social Theory: Making Connections*, Policy Press, Bristol.

Gelb, M. (2004) *How to Think Like Leonardo da Vinci*, Thorsons, London.

Gerdes, K. E. and Segal, E. A. (2009) 'A social work model of empathy', *Advances in Social Work*, Vol. 1, No. 2.

Gerdes, K. and Segal, E. (2011) 'Importance of empathy for social work practice: Integrating new science', *Social Work*, April, Vol. 56, No. 2, pp. 141–148.

Ghaye, T., Lillyman, S. and Gillespie, D. (Eds.) (2000) *Empowerment through Reflection*, Mark Allen Publishing, London.

Giddens, A. and Sutton, P. W. (2013) *Sociology*, Polity Press, Cambridge.

Giddens, A. (1984) *The Constitution of Society: Outline of the Theory of Structuration*, University of California Press, Berkeley.

Giddens, A. (1990). *The Consequences of Modernity*. Stanford, Stanford University Press.

Giddens, A. (1991). *Modernity and Self-Identity: Self and Society in the Late Modern Age*. Cambridge, Polity.

Gillett, W., Bradfield, J. and Nyland, J. (2011) *The Cost of Quality Service Standards: Assessment and Compliance Reporting*, Breaking New Ground, Bradfield Nyland Group and BNG NGO Services Online, Queensland.

Gould, N and Taylor, I. (1996), Reflective Learning for Social Work: Research, Theory and Practice, Arena.

Grant, D. and Oswick, C. (1996) *Metaphor and Organizations*, Sage Publications, London.

Greenfield, S. (2008) *The Quest for Identity in the 21st Century*, Sceptre, London.

Gustar, G. (2014) How might creative writing improve reflective practice amongst managers? OUBS Alumni Careers Network Industry Insights.

Han, S. (2010) 'Theorizing new media: Reflexivity, knowledge, and the Web 2.0*', *Sociological Inquiry*, Vol. 80, pp. 200–213.

Hargreaves, K. (2016) 'Reflection in medical education', *Journal of University Teaching & Learning Practice*, 13(2). Available at: http://ro.uow.edu.au/jutlp/vol13/iss2/6.

Harvey, D. (2005) *A Brief History of Neo-liberalism*, Oxford University Press.

Healy, K. (2014) *Social Work Theories in Context: Creating Frameworks for Practice*, Palgrave, Basingstoke.

Healy, K. (2005) *Social Work Theories in Context*, Palgrave, London.

Heaphy, B. (2007). *Late Modernity and Social Change: Reconstructing Social and Personal Life*. Abington, Routledge.

Hegar, R. L. (2008) 'Transatlantic transfers in social work: Contributions of three pioneers', *British Journal of Social Work*, Vol. 38, No. 4, pp. 716–733.

Hoff, E. (2013) 'The relationship between pretend play and creativity', in M. Taylor (Ed.), *The Oxford Handbook of the Development of Imagination*, Oxford University Press, Oxford.

Holmes, J. (2004) 'Foreword', in J. Kanter (Ed.), *Face to Face with Children, The Life and Work of Clare Winnicott*, Karnac Press, London.

Huang, Y.-T. and L. Fang (2015). "Understanding Depression from Different Paradigms: Toward an Eclectic Social Work Approach." *British Journal of Social Work.*

Hughes, M. and Wearing, M. (2007) *Social Work in Organisations*, Sage Publications, London.

Hurd, F. and Dyer, S. (2017) '"We're all in this together"? The search for collective belonging in a globalised single industry town', *International Journal of Sociology and Social Policy,* Vol. 37, pp. 106–122.

Hynes, P., Lamb, M., Short, D. and Waites, M. (2012) 'Editorial foreword', *Sociology,* Vol. 46, pp. 787–796.

Ife, J. (1997). *Rethinking Social Work: Towards Critical Practice.* Melbourne: Longman.

Ife, J. (2008) *Human Rights and Social Work; Towards Rights Based Practice,* Cambridge University Press, Cambridge.

Inglis, D. (2012) *An Invitation to Social Theory,* Polity Press, Cambridge.

Jackson, N. and Burgess, H. (2005) *Creativity in Social Work and Social Work Education,* Disciplinary Perspectives on Creativity in Higher Education, The Higher Education Academy.

Kanter, J. (1996) 'Introduction to communicating with children' by Clare Winnicott, *Smith College Studies in Social Work,* March, Vol. 66, No. 2.

Kanter, J. (Ed.) (2004) *Face to Face with Children, The Life and Work of Clare Winnicott,* Karnac Press, London.

King Jr., S. (2011) 'The structure of empathy in social work practice', *Journal of Human Behavior in the Social Environment,* Vol. 21, No. 6, pp. 679–695.

Köhler, O., et al. (2016). "The Effect of Concomitant Treatment With SSRIs and Statins: A Population-Based Study." *American Journal of Psychiatry* 173(8): 807–815.

Koht, H. *Presentation Speech by Halvdan Koht,* member of the Nobel Committee, on December 10, 1931. Available at: http://www.nobelprize.org/nobel_prizes/peace/laureates/1931/press.html. Accessed on 11th March, 2017.

Krueger, R. B. (2016) 'Diagnosis of hypersexual or compulsive sexual behavior can be made using ICD-10 and DSM-5 despite rejection of this diagnosis by the American Psychiatric Association', *Addiction,* Vol. 111, pp. 2110–2111.

Krznaric, R. (2008) *You Are Therefore I Am,* Oxfam GB Research Report, UK.

Kuhlmann, C. (2008) 'Alice Salomon (Germany), President 1928/29–1946', *Social Work and Society, International Journal Online.* Available at: http://www.socwork.net/sws/article/view/99/388. Accessed on 11th March, 2017.

Kuhn, D. (1999). A developmental model of critical thinking. Educational Researcher, 28, 16–25.

Laqueur, H. (2015) 'Uses and abuses of drug decriminalization in Portugal', *Law & Social Inquiry,* Vol. 40, pp. 746–781.

Lash, S. (2001) 'Technological forms of life', *Theory, Culture & Society,* Vol. 18, pp. 105–120.

Lee, J. A. B. (1994) *The Empowerment Approach to Social Work Practice,* Columbia University Press, New York.

Letherby, G. (2003). *Feminist research in theory and practice.* Philadelphia, PA, Open University Press.

Lopez, J. (2003) *Society and Its Metaphors – Language, Social Theory and Social Structure*, Continuum, New York and London.

Lukes, S. (1973) *Emile Durkheim, His Life and Work, A Historical and Critical Study,* The Penguin Press, London.

Lundberg, C. (1991) 'Musings on self, culture, and inquiry', in Chapter 25, P. Frost, L. Moore, M. Louis, C. Lundberg and J. Martin (Eds.), *Reframing Organizational Culture,* Sage Publications, London.

MacLean, V. and Williams, J. (2012) 'Ghosts of sociologies past: Settlement sociology in the progressive era at the Chicago School of Civics and Philanthropy', *The American Sociologist*, Vol. 43, pp. 235–263.

Marmot, M. (2016) *2016 Boyer Lecturer: Fair Australia: Social Justice and the Health Gap.* Available at: http://www.abc.net.au/radionational/programs/boyer lectures/series/2016-boyer-lectures/7802472. Accessed on March 19th, 2017.

Martin, J. (2002) *Organizational Culture: Mapping the Terrain*, Sage Publications, Thousand Oaks.

McDonald, C. (2009) 'Critical practice in a changing context', in J. Allan, L. Briskman and B. Pease (Eds.), *Critical Social Work: Theories and Practices for a Socially Just World*, Allen & Unwin, Sydney.

Mead, G. H. (1913) 'The social self', in F. C. Silva (Ed.), *G. H. Mead: A Reader*, Routledge, Abingdon.

Mead, G. H. (1922). A Behavioristic Account of the Significant Symbol. *G. H. Mead: A Reader*. F. C. Silva. London, Routledge.

Mead, G. H. (1925). The Genesis of the Self and Social Control. *G.H. Mead: A Reader*. F. C. Silva. Abingdon, Routledge.

Mead, G. H. (1929) 'The nature of the past', in F. C. Silva (Ed.), *G. H. Mead: A Reader*, Routledge, London.

Miehls, D. and K. Moffatt (2000). "Constructing social work identity based on the reflexive self." *British Journal of Social Work* 30(3): 339–348.

Mills, C. W. (1970) *The Sociological Imagination,* Pelican/Penguin Books, Harmondsworth.

Mohr, G. (2006) 'Dynamic organisational analysis', in G. Mohr and T. Steinert (Eds.), *Growth and Change for Organisations, Transactional Analysis*, International Transactional Analysis Association, Pleasanton.

Moon, J. (2004) *A Handbook of Reflective and Experimental Learning,* Routledge Farmer, London and New York.

Morgan, G. (1986) *Images of Organization,* Sage Publications, Beverly Hills.

Morgan, G. (1993) *Imagination: The Art of Creative Management,* Sage Publishers, London.

Morgan, G. (2006) *Images of Organization,* Barrett-Koehler Publishers, Inc., Sage Publications, Thousand Oaks.

Mullaly, B. (1997) *Structural Social Work – Ideology, Theory and Practice*, Second Edition, Oxford University Press, Ontario.

Munro, E. (2011). The Munro Review of Child Protection: Final Report. A *child-centred System*. UK Government.

Munro, E. (2011), The Munro Review of Child Protection Interim Report: The Child's Journey, London, Department for Education. Available at: http://www.education.gov.uk/munroreview/

Muntaner, C., et al. (2013). Social Stratification, Social Closure, and Social Class as Determinants of Mental Health Disparities. *Handbook of the Sociology of Mental Health*. C. S. Aneshensel, J. C. Phelan and A. Bierman. Dordrecht, Springer Netherlands: 205–227.

Nakamura, J. and Csikszentmihalyi, M. (2002) *The Concept of Flow, Handbook of Positive Psychology*, pp. 89–105. Available at: http://eweaver.myweb.usf.edu/2002-Flow.pdf. Accessed on 2nd February, 2017.

Nisbet, R. A. (1966) *The Sociological Tradition*, Heinemann Educational Books Ltd., London.

Nussbaum, M. (1997) *Cultivating Humanity*, Harvard University Press, Cambridge.

Oswick, C. and Grant, D. (2016) 'Re-imagining images of organization: A conversation with Gareth Morgan'. *Journal of Management Inquiry*, 25 (3) pp. 338–343.

Perron, C. (1970) *Organizational Analysis: A Sociological View*, Wadsworth, Belmont.

Plummer, K. (2010) 'Generational sexualities, subterranean traditions, and the hauntings of the sexual world: Some preliminary remarks', *Symbolic Interaction*, Vol. 33, pp. 163–190.

Reynaud, M., Karila, L., Blecha, L. and Benyamina, A. (2010) 'Is love passion an addictive disorder?', *The American Journal of Drug and Alcohol Abuse,* Vol. 36, pp. 261–267.

Roer, D. (2009) 'Biography work: Reflections on reconstructive social work', *Journal of Social Work Practice,* Vol. 23, No. 2, pp. 185–199.

Rowling J. K. (2000) *The Goblet of Fire*. Bloomsbury Publishing PLC, London.

Ruch, G. and Julkenen, I. (Eds.) (2016) *Relationship-based Research in Social Work: Understanding Practice Research*, Jessica Kingsley, London.

Salomon, A. (2004) 1872–1948. *Character Is Destiny: The Autobiography of Alice Salomon*, University of Michigan Press, Ann Arbor (Edited by Andrew Lees).

Saltiel, D. (2016) 'Observing front line decision making in child protection', *British Journal of Social Work* Vol. 46, No. 7, pp. 2104–2119.

Schaub, J., Willis, P. and Dunk-West, P. (2016) 'Accounting for self, sex and sexuality in UK social workers' knowledge base: Findings from an exploratory study', *British Journal of Social Work* Vol. 47, No. 2, pp. 427–446.

Schwartz, W. (1979) In Compton, B. and Galaway, B. (Eds.), *Social Work Processes,* Dorsey Press, Homewood.

Sewell, W. (1992) 'A theory of structure: Duality, agency, and transformation', *American Journal of Sociology,* Vol. 98, pp. 1–29.

Shaw, I. (2014) 'Sociological social work: A cartoon', *European Journal of Social Work,* Vol. 17, No. 5, pp. 754–770, DOI: 10.1080/13691457.2014.932274.

Sibeon, R. (1991) 'The construction of a contemporary sociology of social work', Chapter Two in Davies, M. (Ed.), *The Sociology of Social Work*, Routledge, London.

Spolander, G., Engelbrecht, L., Martin, L. Strydom, M., Pervova, I., Marjanen, P., Tani, P., Sicora, A. and Adaikalam, F. (2014) 'The implications of neo-liberalism for social work: Reflections from a six-country international research collaboration', *International Social Work*, Vol. 57, No. 4, pp. 301–312.

Stevens, A. and Boladeras, R. (2010) *Developing the Usefulness of Reflective Practice for Professional Development from within eLearning*, Published as part of the Good Practice Publication Grant eBook *(pp.1–11)*. www.akoaotearoa.ac.nz/gppg-ebook. Accessed between July 2016 and November 2017.

Stiles, J. and Jernigan, T. (2010) 'The basics of brain development', *Neuropsychology Review*, Vol. 20, pp. 327–348.

Stupple, E. J. N., Maratos, F. A., Elander, J., Hunt, T. E., Cheung, K. Y. F. and Aubeeluck, A. V. (2017) 'Development of the Critical Thinking Toolkit (CriTT): A measure of student attitudes and beliefs about critical thinking', *Thinking Skills and Creativity*, Vol. 23, pp. 91–100.

Taylor, C. (2004) *Modern Social Imaginaries*, Duke University Press, Durham.

Thody, P. (1993) *The Conservative Imagination*, Pinter Publishers, London.

Thomas, N. (1999) 'Are theories of imagery theories of imagination? An active perception approach to conscious mental content', *Cognitive Science*, Vol. 23, pp. 207–245.

Uglow, J. (2002) *The Lunar Men,* Faber and Faber Limited, London.

Urry, J. (2005) 'The complexities of the global', *Theory, Culture & Society*, Vol. 22, pp. 235–254.

van Wormer, K. (2002) 'Our social work imagination: How social work has not abandoned its mission', *Journal of Teaching in Social Work,* Vol. 22, No. 3/4, pp. 21–36.

Verity, F. (2011) 'Community Development-in the market's slipstream' in J. P. Rothe., L. Carroll, and D. Ozegovic (eds.), *Deliberations on Community Development* Nova Science Publishers: New York.

Verity, F. (2005) *Insurance and Risk Management: Unravelling Civil Society?,* Department of Social Administration and Social Work, Flinders University. Pages 1–37.

Wacquant, L. (2010) 'Crafting the neo-liberal state: Workfare, prisonfare and social insecurity', *Sociological Forum*, Vol. 25, No. 2, June 2010, pp. 197–220.

Weber, M. (1904/1930) *The Protestant Ethic and the Spirit of Capitalism* (Translated by T. Parsons), The Citadel Press, New York.

Wegerif, R. (2010) *Mind Expanding: Teaching for Thinking and Creativity in Primary Education*, Open University Press, Maidenhead.

Weiler, J. (2017) *Alice Salomon*, Jewish Women's Archive. Available at: https://jwa.org/encyclopedia/article/salomon-alice. Accessed on 11th March, 2017.

West, B. (2015) *Re-enchanting Nationalisms: Rituals and Remembrances in a Postmodern Age*, Springer, Berlin.

Weston, S. (2016) 'The everyday work of the drug treatment practitioner: The influence and constraints of a risk-based agenda', *Critical Social Policy*, Vol. 36, pp. 511–530.

Wieler, J. (1988) 'Alice Salomon', *Journal of Teaching in Social Work*, Vol. 2, No. 2, pp. 165–171.

Williams, F. (1999) 'Good-enough principles for welfare', *Journal of Social Policy*, Vol. 28, No. 4, pp. 667–668.

Willis, E. (1999) *The Sociological Quest,* Allen and Unwin, St Leonards.

Winnicott, C. (1977) 'Communicating with children-II', Chapter Nine, in J. Kanter (Ed.), *Face to Face with Children: The Life and Work of Clare Winnicott*, Karnac Books, London.

Winterson, J. (1995) Art Objects: Essays on Ecstatsy and Effrontery, Jonathan Cape: London.

Index

activism   10, 13–14, 116
actor   56–57, 60, 72, 79, 123, 125
Addams, Jane   4–5, 7, 8–22, 24, 36,
   41, 46, 50, 52, 65, 84, 110
advocacy   27, 107

Bauman, Zygmunt   2, 9, 20, 27,
   70–71, 84
Beck, Ulrich   9, 76
Bryson, Lois   4, 32, 39, 73, 78

Chicago School of Sociology   9, 11–12
class   1, 4, 14, 41–42, 62–63, 73, 75,
   90, 106, 110
communication   17, 20, 28, 54, 57,
   83, 91, 103–104, 119
community   1–2, 4, 6, 10–11, 13,
   20–21, 31–32, 35, 41, 48, 52, 54,
   57, 59, 65, 68, 70, 72, 78–79, 84,
   97, 99, 102, 115, 118, 124–125
community development   4, 10–11,
   13, 21, 35, 97, 99
consent   119
contemporary life   81–83
counselling   67, 69, 92
creativity   27–29, 36, 38, 40–44,
   50–51, 124; see also imagination
critical social work   62, 108
   feminist social work theory   5
Csikszentmihalyi, Mihaly   43
cultural capital   65, 73
cultural contexts
culture   1–2, 5, 8, 29, 40, 59, 61, 68,
   75, 83, 96, 98, 102, 114
   individualised culture   74, 76
   modern culture   69; see also
   modernity
   organisational culture   102, 103
   popular culture   66, 69

pre modern culture   69
therapeutic culture   67–68; see also
   socio-cultural

Da Vinci, Leonardo   26, 45
data   70, 90, 99, 11–120
   big data   120
Dialogical   46–47
Dickinson, Emily   24
domestic violence   75

ecological perspective   101–103, 108
emancipatory social work
   practice   107
empathy   17, 19, 22, 24, 27–29, 33,
   36–37, 45, 47, 105, 118, 124
employment   11, 25, 62, 68, 84, 126;
   see also unemployment
empowerment   30, 32, 47, 61, 64,
   105, 108, 125
epistemology   7, 112, 115
ethics   2, 82–83, 103, 111, 120, 121,
   126
ethnography   118
everyday life   34, 45, 66, 100, 118

family   14, 17–18, 21–22, 31, 34, 50,
   54, 72–73, 78, 124
feminist approaches   5, 10, 63
focus groups   118

Gates Starr, Ellen   36
Gender   1, 4, 62–63, 69, 74–75, 83,
   90, 103, 116–117
Generations   10, 21, 90
Giddens, Anthony   8, 57, 60, 62, 69,
   75, 87
Globalisation   15, 20, 83–84, 122
Government   77, 99, 101

human rights   23, 30–31, 51, 81–84
humanistic approaches   67

identity   4, 20, 53–64, 65, 69–70, 75,
    83, 85, 92, 105, 113, 117, 125;
    see also self
imagination   1, 5–8, 15–16, 19,
    23–37, 38–52, 59, 72, 107,
    119, 124
  sociological imagination   2, 5,
    23–37, 38–52, 68, 76, 96,
    116–117, 123–124
inequality   5–6, 9, 12, 21, 32, 46, 57,
    61, 107, 112, 116–117, 121
interactionism *see* symbolic
    interactionism; *see also* Mead,
    George Herbert
internet technology   71, 91, 104,
    119–120
intersectionality   63
intervention   61, 66, 102, 115
interviews   118–119

language   40, 47, 73, 78, 99, 101–102,
    107
lobbying   11

Mead, George Herbert   56–60
metaphor   38–40, 97–109
Mills, C. Wright   24, 27, 34, 38, 44,
    52, 96
Morgan, Gareth   6
Morris, William   36, 42, 44, 48
Munro, Eileen   39–40, 91

normative   31, 65, 85
Nussbaum, Martha   25, 29, 77

oppression   9, 51, 57, 106

parenting   119
policy   2–4, 27, 35, 39, 79, 83–85,
    115
popular culture, *see* culture

population   117
professional self-making   59, 63
psychoanalytic theory   9, 19, 55,
    58–60, 67
psycho-social   123

race   1, 4, 7, 29, 63, 103; *see also*
    culture
reflexivity   58–60, 62–64, 125
religion   29, 63
resilience   68
risk   9, 66, 87, 94, 99, 108, 126
Rogers, Carl   4, 67

Salomon, Alice   6, 8, 16–22, 34–35,
    38, 45, 48, 50, 65, 84, 110
self   2, 53–61, 67
self determination   6, 53, 60–61
sexual identity   61, 83
social imaginary   24, 30–31, 36, 45,
    51, 81, 122
social justice   2–3, 6, 9–10, 20–21, 23,
    29–32, 51, 58, 85, 107, 109, 116,
    127
socio-cultural   25, 123
sociological imagination *see*
    imagination
social work ethics *see* ethics

Taylor, Charles   6, 30
technology   20, 71, 77, 83, 91, 93,
    104–106, 109

unemployment   70

van Wormer, Katherine   4, 6, 10, 15,
    24, 26–28, 34–35, 40, 46, 51

Weber, Max   6, 38–39, 63, 95, 106
Winnicott, Clare   5, 8–9, 17–22, 28,
    33, 36, 51, 65
women   8, 10, 11, 14–15, 41, 61,
    74–75, 77, 87, 116–119; *see also*
    gender

Printed by Printforce, the Netherlands